HOW TO BE AN
ENTREPRENEUR

HOW TO BE AN ENTREPRENEUR

A GUIDE FOR THE UNDER 25s

IAN PHILLIPSON

KOGAN
PAGE

First published in 1995

Kogan Page Limited
120 Pentonville Road
London N1 9JN

© Ian Phillipson 1995

British Library Cataloguing in Publication Data

A CIP record for this book is available from the British Library.

ISBN 0-7494-1554-1

Printed and bound in Great Britain by
Biddles Ltd, Guildford and King's Lynn

Contents

Preface

The early 1990s recession has ingrained itself into the working psyche of the country, and has fundamentally changed attitudes to work. There are no such things as jobs for life any more. Even traditionally safe areas such as the Civil Service, the armed services and banking have seen massive jobs losses over recent years. Workers have had to become more self-reliant, and none more so than those just setting out on their working lives: the school and college leavers.

Work patterns too are changing. People are no longer content to do a nine-to-five job, with little variety all their lives like their parents did. School and college leavers will have been used to, over their student years, a very different working pattern from traditional employed work and will be unwilling to give it up.

Many such school and college leavers, as well as young people in and out of employment, are turning to the idea of starting their own business and keeping their fate in their own hands. The entrepreneurial spirit of the 1980s is alive and well in the 1990s, though its excesses have been tamed. But they will quite naturally be asking themselves whether they have what it takes; whether they can succeed; how exactly they start about going into business; and whether they can deal with all those matters such as finance and marketing for which little in their education will have prepared them.

This book specifically answers these questions and more for the under-25s, acknowledging and suggesting solutions to the special problems of the younger entrepreneur.

Good luck.

1

Why be an Entrepreneur?

It's a magnificent word, isn't it? Entrepreneur. It rolls around the mouth, sounds exotic and suggests wealth. Can't you just imagine telling people you're 'an entrepreneur'? Well, let's hope so because you can be.

But what exactly is an entrepreneur? What do you have to do to become one? When do you become one? What does an entrepreneur *do*? This book will answer these questions and more. However, it's rather different from the usual 'starting up in business' books for a number of reasons.

First, this book works from the basic viewpoint that being an entrepreneur is often an immensely personal thing that requires *you* to develop certain characteristics and skills, and to rid yourself of others. For that reason there is a concentration on topics not ordinarily included in business books particularly self-management (if you can't manage yourself then you won't do well in business) and image creation (looking business-like improves your chances of doing business). In particular, *How to be an Entrepreneur* describes techniques and offers information that is of particular help to the younger entrepreneur.

If you've been interested in starting your own business for a while, you will probably already have browsed through, borrowed or bought books on how to do it. There are lots around, many of them very good, but nearly all suffer from one major defect: they try to be all things to all people. Well, if you are under 25, this book talks specifically to you. It takes a realistic approach to what, as a relative youngster you can realistically achieve immediately and how you can overcome the barriers that are stacked against you because of your age.

Consequently, *How to be an Entrepreneur* ignores some major aspects of running a business. You won't find anything here on setting up account books, cash flows or the differences between 'sole trader', 'partnerships' or 'limited liability companies'. The reason? Again, there are already perfectly adequate books on these subjects, so why duplicate effort?

Who this book is for

If you are interested in business but are still at school or college; if you are just about to leave school or college; if you are already working either part-time or full-time; or if you are unemployed and think setting up your own business is a way forward, then this book is for you.

And as *How to be an Entrepreneur* is written as a *practical* guide you'll be asked to do a few practical things. The first of these is to take a trip down to the shops to buy yourself a hard-backed notebook of ruled paper. This will be your companion as you read because in it you'll be making lists, answering questions about yourself, jotting down thoughts as they occur to you and planning your business strategy. This will be your 'Entrepreneur's Book' and it provides you with just one reference source, rather than having 40 to 50 sheets of loose paper floating around.

Right, you're back from the shops with your book, which you are going to use immediately by answering the question below.

What is an entrepreneur?

What do *you* mean by an entrepreneur? Write down your definition but don't try and strive for a perfect definition. Just let your mind search for the different characteristics *you* associate with an entrepreneur. Give yourself five minutes to do this. Do it now.

The *Shorter Oxford Dictionary* defines an entrepreneur as 'a person who undertakes or controls a business or enterprise and bears the risk of profit or loss'. Well, it's a starting point.

But like many dictionary definitions it's a bit broad and does not tell you very much. For instance, it suggests anyone who runs a business is an entrepreneur ... do you think that? Is the local fishmonger handing over a pound of cod to Mrs Johnson and asking about her varicose veins an entrepreneur? To the dictionary he may be, but not in real life.

Take a look at your definition of an entrepreneur. Unless you sneaked a peek at the dictionary before starting the chances are that your definition won't be anything like the dictionary's. Right? Instead, you'll probably have jotted down words like ambition, energy, flair, achievement, fast moving, high profile, risk taking, innovative and successful. You were probably thinking of Richard Branson, who is almost the model entrepreneur in most people's eyes. Well, that's my idea of an entrepreneur too. Someone who is always on the look-out for opportunities and who knows how to take risks.

Getting serious

Obviously Branson is something of a one-off. Achieving his heights will be something that only a few can do, but there's no reason at all why you shouldn't set your business sights high. As the saying goes, if you aim for the stars you may only hit the moon, but if you aim for the trees you can only hit the ground.

Setting up and running a business isn't anything special if you put your mind to it, since it is largely about doing things at the right time, in the right way and for the right people. However, the problem is that a lot of young people who could be successful in business don't take the chance because everyone tells them they won't or can't make it. But how will you know if you don't give it a go? So let's give you a confidence boost by exploding some of the 'Myths Others Tell You About Business'. These are just some of the comments that a young would-be entrepreneur can expect from family, relatives and friends.

Myth 1. You need a good education
There you are with just one GCSE and an accent that comes straight out of *Eastenders*: what chance do you stand? Well plenty, *if* you are determined enough to overcome your

shortcomings. It's true, business life can be that much easier if you do have a good education behind you. For one thing, you'll find it easier to convince others that you know what you are doing. If you can flourish a fistful of exam certificates in their face then they will assume that you are intelligent. A good education can also give you confidence because you have this wider breadth of formal knowledge.

However, there are plenty of people with good educations failing in business, and there are those with lousy educations under their belts who end up millionaires. But there is one important element that you should not forget. A good entrepreneur always keeps on learning. Sure, they weren't any good at history and didn't know one end of a French verb from another, but when it comes to learning more about selling, customer psychology or new marketing techniques they never stop. Any business person who says that they know everything about their industry or profession is a fool. So, if you do not have a good education behind you, don't worry, you can still make it.

Myth 2. You have to be clever

Realistically, not being able to walk and chew gum at the same time would be a major blow to anyone's business career; however, that doesn't mean you need a sky-high IQ either or to be academically gifted; but you do need to be mentally alert. Of two entrepreneurs, one a lazy so-and-so but is bright enough to do *The Times* crossword in ten minutes without trying, and another who has a burning ambition to succeed and works all hours God sends, I know who my money would be on to come out best entrepreneur! And don't think that there is only one type of intelligence. You may be good at taking IQ tests, but being able to 'read' people, or spot an opportunity, are really specific forms of intelligence that are far more important in achieving business success.

Myth 3. You need money

It can't be denied, having a million pounds in the bank to back your business ambitions does give you something of a headstart because it provides you with all sorts of options you would not otherwise have. Not only do more business opportunities open up, but you have the bankroll to move things forward quickly, which can be crucial: so many good businesses fail early simply because their owners don't have the capital that lets them expand at the right moment or to ride out a rough patch.

However, most people don't have a million down at the Midland, so what can you do? Well, you start lower down the scale, setting up a business that doesn't need a huge bank balance to get going. When that's successful you use it to finance another business. In the end you do have a million in the bank. Money helps but it's not an essential if you are flexible.

Myth 4. You need a brilliant idea

Every business depends on an initial idea. Some of these are better than others. But though the idea you come up with is important, often more important is what you do with the idea. How hard are you prepared to work at making the idea succeed? How good will you be at overcoming problems when they arise? How enthusiastic are you at developing the idea? There are lots of frustrated would-be entrepreneurs out there just waiting for the perfect idea to come along. It rarely does, so don't be one of them. Get stuck in.

Myth 5. You need to be ruthless

JR Ewing in *Dallas*, Michael Douglas as Gordon Gecko in *Wall Street*, Mike Baldwin in *Coronation Street* ... are these the ruthless business people we're talking about? Don't you just love those who have fought, kicked and punched their way up the business world without a scruple? Sorry, but the business world isn't all like that; though of course there will always be bad guys around who work their staff in sweatshops for all hours of the day and night, go home, eat ground glass for supper and then bankrupt a business rival before bedtime. It would be naive to suggest that skulduggery doesn't play a part in the business world, but business is rarely conducted like this. While there is no need to be ruthless, you do need a watered-down cousin of ruthlessness, namely determination. You need to make sure that people don't play you for a sucker, while you persuade people to do what you want them to. You can do that if you're a normal person; you don't need veins filled with iced water.

Eight reasons not to be in business when you're young

You should be feeling a little more confident by now that you can make a success of business, but you mustn't forget that there are some real disadvantages to being young. Some of them can be difficult to counter.

1. When you start you will have to do everything yourself; that means long hours, long hours and more long hours. That can be something of a shock after the relaxed nature of school, college and unemployment. Are you up to it?

2. Whatever your age there's an element of risk in being in business as there's no guaranteed income at the end of every week or month as there is when you are in salaried employment. At the same time, you have people hounding you to pay your monthly bills. That all adds to the pressure and stress you will feel. Can you take it?

3. When you are young and in business you will have to deal with the 'I didn't get where I am today dealing with young whippersnappers' attitude from older business people and suppliers, particularly men. They have served an 'apprenticeship' working their way up the system over 20 or 30 years to reach where they are. Because of their own irrational prejudices they will distrust you and resent your efforts.

4. Other business people will tend not to take you seriously because of your age. And if you look as though you are only 16, even though you are 22, that can be off-putting to a business person who is 40 years your senior.

5. When you are young, people will say you are and expect you to be inexperienced. Being inexperienced means that you aren't up to the job, are likely to let them down, cause them problems or not have the technical ability they're

looking for. If their hard-earned money rides on the actions of someone they think inexperienced, they may ultimately play safe and give the work to someone they regard as being more experienced and better able to do the job. For that reason you will have to work harder and harder to prove to them that you are professional, can meet deadlines and do what you say you will do. Don't be resentful if you are even asked for references; think of this as the customer being interested in what you have to offer.

6. When you are young you may not be able to charge as much for your services or product. Customers or clients will bargain hard with you, knowing that you probably need the business. Worse still, you may be aware of your own weakness in this area and consequently ask for less than you should. This is a problem for everyone starting up a new business, whatever their age.

7. When you are young an awareness of your own inexperience means that you tend to lack confidence in yourself which is reflected in your business dealings. People may think that they can rip you off.

8. Because you have been in business, others may see you as unemployable later on if you need a job. They may think you are too independent and not a team player, won't be able to take orders from anyone else. They may also say to themselves, 'You obviously can't be a good business person, or you wouldn't want a job with me now'.

Thirteen reasons to be in business when you're young

1. You have always wanted to be an entrepreneur when others wanted to be train drivers or nurses. This is one of the best reasons you can have.

2. There are no other options for you. The workplace is changing fast, especially for young people, and as the traditional avenues of employment close down, self-employment looks an increasingly interesting option for the under-25s.

3. You have what you think is a profitable idea or you see an opportunity that you want to exploit. Every business starts with an idea.

4. You think you will have more independence than you would otherwise. You won't have to do what others tell you and you can be master or mistress of your own decisions. All true.

5. You have acquired skills, ideas and knowledge that you think you can put to very good effect in the business world.

6. You'll feel more secure running your own business rather than working as an employee for someone else. To some that may seem strange, but think about it. Can you be secure in any job today when you are always looking over your shoulder waiting for the redundancy notice? These days there are no jobs for life.

7. As a business person, if things aren't going well you can do something about it through your own efforts, working longer or being smarter. If you are an employee you may disagree with management's decisions yet be unable to do anything about them.

8. You have far greater control over what you do. If something is unproductive or a waste of time you can cut it out of your day. This means that you can end up with a far better lifestyle by having a better car, when you want it, taking a holiday when you want it (as long as all of these are possible). At the same time you will have freedom to go down routes and avenues that are closed when working as an employee.

9. As a young person you can bring a whole range of ideas and thoughts to the business world. This lets you take a fresh look at the business world and see opportunities and chances that older, more jaded people just don't see. Most importantly, you probably won't think that there is just one way to do things as so many older business people do.

You will also have a greater awareness of what people of your own age want. In business, the older and more successful you become, the easier it is to become isolated from the world at large, particularly the younger markets. Carving out a business niche selling to people you understand and can empathise with could be a highly profitable move. Why not exploit that market while you still have a very good knowledge of it?

10. You may well know more about modern technology than older business people, be less frightened of using it and also see opportunities to exploit it. This isn't to suggest that you're some 'tech-head', but someone who understands that technology is there to be used even if you don't necessarily understand its fine workings.

11. As a young entrepreneur you should have a lot of energy and good health so you are able to work longer and harder than someone twice your age.

12. At your age you should be hungry for success, while many older business people will have reached a level of comfort and stopped there, no longer willing to work the hours or surmount yet another problem.

13. And last but certainly not least, because you want to make money. Remember, you don't make serious money working for someone else.

What skills do you need to succeed?

It's all very well saying you want to go into business for yourself, but there have to be some particular skills that are useful to have. These skills are listed below.

A willingness to make things happen
As an entrepreneur everything in your business will revolve around you and if you don't do things, they won't happen. Wishful thinking has no place in the armoury of the entrepreneur. So, once you have an idea, you must support it by doing all the things that you need to.

One further point: a willingness to do things also involves a willingness to do the bad things that are no fun and cause you grief, the things you don't like doing but still need to be done. You won't be able to put off this bad stuff, especially when there is no one else around to help you.

Energy and drive
This factor is very much linked to the point above. If you have to give up on something after you've only been doing it for half an hour because you can't motivate yourself, you will always lose out to the person who can. Obviously, you will have more energy and drive if you are fit and healthy, and you'll need it, especially if you are going into a physically demanding type of business. When you link energy and drive with a willingness to do things, then you have persistence, something that all entre- preneurs need.

Self-confidence
It isn't necessary to have an extrovert personality that lets you strip naked in public or dance on restaurant tables, but you do need quite an outgoing character. As an entrepreneur you oper- ate in the real world where mummy can't hold your hand. Shrinking violets lose out. Therefore you will need to have confidence in your own abilities (you won't be very successful if you think you can't do things very well); you need to have confidence in your decision-making powers (it's no good if every time you make a choice you think it will be the wrong one); and you need to have the confidence to fail.

The ability to spot business opportunities
Of course, you can set up any old business and run it day to day, keeping things on an even keel, not rocking the boat, steady as she goes, just like the fishmonger we met above. But that's not very entrepreneurial and all it's going to get you is a business that just about makes you a living. If you want to get on you must know how to develop other ways of making money by spotting and seizing opportunities. The world today is a fast changing one and if you don't look for other opportu-

nities you will soon find that what you thought was a secure business venture is now old fashioned and behind the times.

The ability to seize business opportunities

Seeing a gap in the market is no good if you don't do anything about it. There are people out there, seeing out their retirement on a state pension, telling anyone who will listen that they thought of the Black and Decker Workmate (a major best-selling product) five years before it was invented. Don't be like them. Entrepreneurs aren't. If they think their idea is a good one they don't wait around, but go for it.

The ability to take risks

At some point in business you also have to take a chance if you want to move up a level. Of course you do everything you can to erase unnecessary risk but some risk is inevitable. The real skill here is the ability to tell the difference between what is an acceptable risk and what is not.

The ability to organise resources

Give two different people exactly the same money, equipment and idea and you would have two different results, one more successful than the other. When you are young the fewer resources, financial and otherwise, you are likely to have so the more you can use what little you have the better.

A money mentality

Not every business person sets out to make money from their work; some just see it as a means of creating a job for themselves. However, if you do want to increase your chance of being successful then you have to think in terms of money. This doesn't mean that you suddenly become a horrible person or are motivated by pure greed. No, just as footballers keep a tally of all the goals they score, so a successful business person will see money as a way of keeping score of their success.

Persuasive powers

The ability to get others to do what you want them to do is a great ability in all walks of life, but especially so in the business world, because it's a crucial skill in important areas such as selling and negotiating. It can mean the difference between success and failure. So a good level of social skills is a great asset. If you don't have them you will have to acquire them.

Communication skills
Very much linked to the above is an ability to communicate with others, both in the spoken and written word. Good writing skills are often underestimated, but are essential in the business world.

High personal goals
Ideally, you should set yourself a very high standard in all that you do, and not just business dealings. The higher you aim, the more likely you are to succeed. It also means that you push yourself harder to reach your self-imposed goals.

A positive attitude to life
Having a positive mental attitude to life means that even when things seem pretty dire and dreadful you can still summon up the enthusiasm to push forward. Of course, you always want to succeed but having a positive mental attitude means that you will always think that it is worth the try.

Decision-making skills
Life is full of choices and you must learn how to choose between them if you are going to be a successful entrepreneur. Often those decisions are very hard and when you have made a decision you need to be able to evaluate your success. Did you make a good decision or a bad one?

A willingness to learn
As mentioned earlier, if you can't be bothered to learn or don't want to make the effort, then, in a changing world, you will be left behind. Every one of us can improve our existing skills and range of knowledge. One of the most important types of learning experience is that of learning from our own mistakes. These are often the most painful, but often the most valuable lessons

that you can have. If you make mistakes but don't learn from them, nothing at all will have been gained from the error but pain ... yours.

Foresight
Being able to look into the future and see what are the up-and-coming opportunities, and what might go wrong, is a valuable ability, because it helps you in working out your long-term plans. It is doubly valuable when linked with the characteristic below.

Adaptability
You never know what the world of business is going to throw at you. One day everything is fine and the next competitors are doing something outrageous, the public seem to have stopped buying your product and you are having problems with a supplier. Knowing how to change your usual way of doing things to cope with changes requires adaptability.

Commitment
If you only give things half a chance and they fail you will never know if they would have worked had you given them your best shot. Good entrepreneurs give their business the best shot even when the hours are long and their only companion is loneliness.

Creativity
You don't need to be a Picasso, but being able to come up with ideas is important. You will need creativity, not just to think up new business ideas, but to adapt old ones to take advantage of changes to your existing circumstances.

Pressure-handling
When you are in business you are generally on your own, reliant on your own efforts and dependent on your own decisions, right or wrong. All of this can create a great deal of stress from time to time, either because things are going so well that you don't know how to cope with all the extra work, or because things are going so badly that you don't know where the next penny is coming from.

Good organisation and administration skills

You may have the most brilliant idea in the world, more than adequate financing and a market just waiting to be milked, but if you can't organise the day-to-day running of a business it will soon run into trouble. Organising your time, making sure things are done when they are meant to be and handling paperwork are all part and parcel of being an entrepreneur.

Attention to detail

Perhaps not the most crucial characteristic you'll need as an entrepreneur but a very important one nevertheless in helping you to ensure that there are no loose ends around to make a project or scheme unravel. If you can think through an idea you will see areas that might cause you problems later.

The above is quite a shopping list and it would be an entrepreneurial superhero who possessed them all in equal degrees. Obviously, the more of these characteristics you have the better off you will be, but don't worry if you have weak areas. The important thing at this point is to know what those weak areas are and begin to strengthen them. This book will help you to do that.

Plan of action

1. Begin reading the business sections of newspapers and business magazines, especially those that are related to self-employment or running a small business. (See sources of information, page 149.)

2. Read books on entrepreneurs such as Victor Kiam (Remington), Richard Branson (Virgin), Anita Roddick (Body Shop) and Sophie Merman (Sock Shop). How did they react in situations, what elements of their character come through? What can you learn from them? Start browsing through the appropriate sections of libraries and bookshops.

3. Begin observing business people. How do they behave? Which ones look successful? Why do they look successful?

4. Look around for a course on how to set up and run a business. Your local TEC or Careers Office should have information on such courses, or Livewire on 0345 573252.

5. If you haven't any business experience, start thinking about where you can gain some. It doesn't matter in what at this stage, but anything with an element of selling or administration would be useful.

   Think about taking a job selling double glazing, encyclopedias or insurance. You won't receive a salary (or if you do it will be very small) as these jobs tend to be commission based, but then you aren't doing it for the money. You only need to stick the job for a few weeks, but it will give you an invaluable insight into how you need to sell to people, overcoming their fears and objections and rejection by them. Selling face to face is a great buzz. You never forget the first time you sell something to a stranger.

6. If you've been unemployed for a while, you will probably have lost confidence in yourself. Understandably, many respond by not doing anything, spending hours and hours just sitting around, watching television and listening to music. All of that is fine, at the right time and in the right place. But if you want to get into business you have to start breaking the 'doing nothing rut' that your body and subconscious mind will have fallen into.

   Start to do things again and as many of them as possible. It doesn't matter what they are, though if you enjoy them so much the better. Offer to do the washing up, mow the lawn, cut the hedges, dig the garden, do the shopping, clean the car, tidy the house, paint a room, take a walk, play football or hockey, go running, or explore a museum.

   Another consequence of this is that, not only are you putting your brain back in gear, but you start impressing others. Look at it this way, your family see that you are beginning to take a direction and be active. Then if in six months time you say, 'I'm going to start a business', they're going to look more sympathetically and perhaps helpfully on you than they would if you had just stumbled off the sofa one day and announced the same thing. Family help can be a great boost in business so don't ignore it, cultivate it.

2

Can You be an Entrepreneur?

This chapter is all about you. It's a hard-work chapter as it calls for you to be honest with yourself, asking questions of your character and personality and answering them truthfully. If you lie, it doesn't matter to anyone else, but it does matter one hell of a lot to you. So, think of this as being a job interview that you are conducting on yourself. Do you get the job?

You'll be asked to look back over the last few years to your school days, college life and early work experience. Your answers should reveal those areas in which you feel comfortable, your skills and your weaknesses. What you do with that information is up to you. Write your responses down in your book. Be as thorough and accurate as you can.

Besides helping to assess your suitability for business life, this chapter serves another purpose. When looking back on what you've done in the past, it's very easy, especially if you are going through a 'bit of a downer', to think that you have achieved nothing in your life. Probably not true. Therefore it is important when completing this self-assessment that you come up with as much detail as possible because the more detail you can remember when answering the questions the greater will be your belief that you *have* achieved things in life. The stronger your belief the greater will be your chances of succeeding in business life.

There are very many people who do not live up to their potential because they have *self-limiting beliefs*, that is *they* tell *themselves* they can't do something. The result: they can't do something, even though they could. Don't be someone with those self-limiting beliefs. Entrepreneurs have to have confidence in themselves and what they can do.

As you work through the questions don't just answer yes or no, but think about what your answer says about you and how the question relates to business. Ask yourself how that skill could be used. You should spend a good hour on your self-assessment and preferably two.

Your daily life

Every one of us has a routine to our lives that reflects our own individual attitudes, ideas and characters. And though some people put their lives in compartments, for instance being highly organised in one area but not in another, most of us carry those characteristics from one area into another. Therefore, what you do in your daily life can suggest what you will or will not be good or bad at in business life.

- What activities in your daily life do you like doing best? List ten. Why do you like these activities particularly?
- What activities in your daily life do you not like doing? List ten. Why do you dislike these activities particularly?
- What activities in your life do you absolutely love doing? List five. Why are these so good?
- What activities in your life do you really hate doing? List five. Why are these so bad?

Your school and college life

You may not have a fully developed character when you are at school, but nevertheless some useful insights into your character should come through which may be of use in an entrepreneurial career.

- What are your exam grades?
- What is/was your best subject and why are/were you so good at it?
- What is/was the subject you enjoy(ed) most and why do/did you enjoy it so much?

- What is/was your worst subject and why are/were you so bad at it?
- What is/was the subject you dislike(d) most and why do/did you dislike it so much?
- What if any, are/were your best sporting achievements? How did you achieve these?
- Did you win any special awards? Why did you win them?
- What clubs are/were you a member of? Why did you choose those clubs?
- Are/were you an official of any of these clubs? Why did you became an official?
- Are/were you frequently suggesting schemes and ideas to others in your class?
- Have you engaged in any trading of 'school currencies' such as books, marbles and sports equipment?
- Do/did you put homework and course work in on time?
- Have you been involved with or submitted material to the school or college newspaper or magazine?

Part-time work

It is as well to start good working habits as early as possible, so that they become exactly that, habits. Part-time work is often done to earn money for something specific, such as a car, CD player or holiday. It is very good experience to link the achievement of a particular goal with earning money. You also learn skills and experiences that stand you in good stead later in your working life.

If you haven't done any part-time work, it is worth asking yourself why. Is it because there is no part-time work around? Were you not sufficiently motivated? A lack of commitment to part-time work may suggest that you may not be 100 per cent committed to being an entrepreneur.

- What part-time work have you done?
- Where do/did you do this part-time work?
- Why work there?
- What have you learned from this work?
- Have you acquired any particular skills or specialised knowledge from it?

Full-time work

Work takes up a third of nearly every day. So what you like and dislike about the work you do should give an indication about what you feel comfortable doing, the situations that you are happy to deal with, and the situations you find difficult to deal with.

- At work, what things do you like doing most?
- At work, what things do you like doing least?
- At work what do other people say you are good at?
- At work what do other people say you are bad at?
- What are the particular characteristics that your job requires? Do you have these characteristics or are you a square peg in a round hole?
- Can you delegate to others jobs that you have to do?
- Can you make decisions about what has to be done?
- Can you use a computer and other modern technology?
- Can you word process or type?
- Are you good with paperwork?
- Have you acquired any specialised knowledge from your work?

Leisure time

Perhaps your education and working life have not so far been perfect, but what about your leisure time? Many people who have not excelled in other fields do so when pursuing their leisure activities, acquiring valuable and useful skills. If you can do that in your leisure-time activities then you can also do that in business.

- What do you do in your spare time?
- What are the skills that your particular hobby requires?
- Are you a member of any clubs outside school and college?
- Have you won a club competition?
- Are you an official of any club? Do you organise events or activities for the club?
- Do you have any achievements in your leisure activities that you are particularly proud about?

● Have you acquired any specialised knowledge from your leisure activities?

Your characteristics

Your personality can have a major impact on your business success. The questions below relate to some of the key characteristics of entrepreneurs outlined in the previous chapter.

A willingness to do things

● Are you able to get done the things you have to do, or do you put them off?

● What was the last thing that you put off doing? What were the consequences of putting it off?

● Are you putting off doing something now? What will be the consequences of doing this?

● Do you make the appointments (dentist, doctor, bank manager) you know you have to, or do you put them off?

● Can you concentrate on what you are doing or does your mind fly away to other things?

● Do you complete homework, college or work projects on time? Do you finish it in time beforehand or have to rush to do it at the last minute?

● If you need a new skill in order to do something, have you gone out and acquired it? When was the last time you did this?

● Have you ever gone out to learn a new language on your own?

Your energy and drive

● Do you normally find you have enough energy to do what you want to do, or are you continually flopped out?

● Do you spend a lot of your spare time slumped in front of the television or are you up and about doing things?

● Would you say that you have a lot of stamina?

Self-confidence

- Do you have confidence in yourself?
- Do you have a bit of an ego and like showing off to people?
- Do you like to tell jokes and stories to a group of friends?
- Have you ever appeared on stage?
- Do you like talking in front of others?
- Can you go on and do something you think right even if others are saying that you are wrong?
- Can you do things on your own, or do you need the moral support of others?
- Can you find out information from people? When was the last time you did this?
- Can you chat up boys/girls?
- If someone asks you to do something you have never done before, do you think of it as a problem, or a new challenge?
- Do you find it fairly easy to work on your own? When was the last time that you had to do this?

Business instinct

Have you ever spotted what you thought was a good business idea?

- Have you ever seen a new product or service and said to yourself, 'I thought of that six months ago?'
- Have you ever had a flash of inspiration in which you've thought to yourself, 'That would make a good business idea'?
- Have you ever said about a business, 'They'd be a lot more successful if they did this or that'?
- Are you interested in what other people are doing?
- Before starting this book, did you read the business pages in newspapers?
- Who are your heroes? Are there any business people among them?

Risk taking

- When have you taken risks? List five examples in the last five years.
- Do you tend to take risks or are you rather cautious by nature?
- If you take risks are they calculated risks or do they tend to be spur-of-the-moment and reckless decisions?
- Do you try out new sports, activities, foods and restaurants?
- When someone asks if you want to do something new, is your immediate reaction normally to say 'yes' or 'no'?

Awareness of money

- Can you balance your cheque book?
- Do you know how much money is in your account at any one time?
- Do you run an unauthorised overdraft?
- Do you get scolding letters from the bank?

Persuasion and communication skills

- Do people say that you write well?
- Do people say that you talk well?
- Do you like reading?
- Can you put a point over well?
- Can you talk to strangers?
- Can you persuade others to do things that they don't really want to do?
- Can you come up with reasons why others should follow your particular idea or course of action rather than someone else's?
- Can you explain things to others clearly so that they understand something they didn't do before? When was the last time you did this?
- Do you get on well with others?
- After you have told or asked someone to do something, are you able to supervise them properly so that they get the job done?

● Have you ever sold anything? When and what was it?

High personal goals

● Do you know what you want out of life?
● Do you reckon that you have high personal goals?
● Do you set goals for yourself?
● Do you meet these goals?
● Do you have any written goals?
● If someone asked you what your aims in life are, could you tell them immediately or would you have to think about it?

Positive attitude to life

● Are you an optimist or a pessimist?
● Are you generally a happy person or someone who is sad?
● If things go against you, does it get you down or do you say, 'Right, I'll show them' and bounce back?

Decision-making skills

● When was the last time you made a decision?
● Do you make decisions very often? Are they big or little decisions?
● Are your decisions generally right or wrong in retrospect?
● Do you think of yourself as being decisive, or do you dither?
● Think of a recent big decision that you had to make.
● Was that decision right? If it was right how did you feel?
● If it was wrong, did you feel like never making another decision again?

Willingness to learn

● When was the last time you made an effort to learn a skill or acquire knowledge that you *didn't have to* for school, work or college?
● You need some information immediately, but aren't at first sure where to obtain it. Can you research and track down

the people who can help you find the information you need or are you left floundering?
● When was the last time you went to a library to find information?

Foresight

● When was the last time you really had to think ahead?
● When you did that and spotted a potential problem, did that give you a buzz?

Adaptability

● When was the last time circumstances made you change your plans where you had to come up with something else fast?
● Can you do more than one thing at once?
● Do you think of yourself as being a flexible and adaptable sort of person? Do others think the same?

Commitment

● When you need to do something can you just sit down and get on with it, no matter what the distractions?
● If you are in the middle of doing something that has to be finished by next morning and a friend drops by to invite you out for the evening, will you go?
● Will you watch your favourite television programme rather than finish off a job you don't like, but one that has to be done?
● When have you worked longer hours than you needed?
● When have you put in extra effort on a job or project?
● Do you tend to start doing things and then leave them unfinished?
● When you set your mind to do something, do you usually finish it?
● When was the last time you really pushed yourself?
● Have you ever participated in an endurance sport such as cross-country, marathon running or the triathlon? Are you involved in a sport for which you train regularly?

Creativity

- When was the last time you did something creative?
- Do others say 'what an imagination you've got'?
- Do you like to do crosswords or puzzles?
- Do you watch quiz programmes on tv?
- Can you come up with new ideas? List the last five times you have done this.
- Can you come up with ideas that solve problems?
- After you have come up with a problem-solving idea, are you able to assess its quality and tell whether it is a good or bad one?
- When you are faced with a problem, do you immediately panic or do you look for a way to solve it?
- Do you write, paint, play music or do anything else that shows a creative talent?

Pressure-handling

- When was the last time you were under real pressure? How did you cope with it?
- When faced with pressure, is your first instinct to run away from the problem?
- Do you conquer this instinct and confront the problem or do you tend to run and let the pressure build up?
- Do you try to let others take the pressure on themselves or do you take responsibility for the situation?

Organisation and administration skills

- Do you plan projects or just let them happen?
- Do you frequently organise systems for doing things?
- Can you plan your day?
- Can you work to a timetable?
- Do you make lists of the things you have to do in the day?
- If you go on holiday or on a trip, do you make a checklist of the things you have to do?
- Do you buy people's birthday presents ahead of time?
- Do you do your Christmas shopping before the rush?

- Do you remember to send forms back on time?
- Do you know when your passport expires?
- Is it left to you to organise events or parties?
- Do you or can you organise what others have to do?
- Have you ever organised a long-term project? When was the last time you did this?

By working through these questions you should have developed a fairly good idea of what your strong points and your weaknesses are.

Now turn back to the previous chapter and compare what you have written with the characteristics of entrepreneurs. Are you exhibiting any of the same ones? If you are, great; it seems that you are heading down the right track. And if you aren't, well it may be that you just aren't cut out to be in business; not everyone is.

However, be positive. This assessment is only an *indication* of what you can do and what you might be like as an entrepreneur. The future is not set in stone, nor does it have to depend wholeheartedly on what you have done in the past. If you want to be successful in business and are determined enough, you will succeed, no matter what you have done, or not done, in the past. It's all down to you.

However, at this stage you might be thinking that you just don't have the character to be in business. Well, that's something in itself and it gives you the opportunity to bail out now, to think no more about going into business and to concentrate on developing another area for yourself.

Plan of action

1. Even though you are not in business yet, start practising some of the skills of entrepreneurship in everyday life, for instance by using your imagination to think up new ideas; becoming more positive in your approach to life; and doing any paperwork you must do on time. Work your way down the 'characteristics' list of Chapter 1 and choose three characteristics that you will make a special effort to develop in your everyday life.

2. If you lack formal education, consider improving it by taking courses at a local adult education college, or using the Open University. Courses on computers, information technology and languages are very useful as knowledge of all three are increasingly important in the business world.

3. Start to become more disciplined about your life in general. In particular, try to do the things that you don't like doing, but which still have to be done.

3

How to Choose Your Business

Every business starts with an idea and the world is full of business ideas and opportunities just waiting to be exploited. But not all of them will fit in with what you want from a business. If you end up choosing a business idea which doesn't meet your expectations, you will become frustrated and the business won't give you what you want from it; indeed it might even fail. So, this chapter is all about choosing a business idea that's right for you, and again you'll have to ask yourself a lot of questions.

What type of business?

1. Do you want a fast-track or a slow-track business? A fast-track business will earn you money quickly, but may only be a short-lived phenomenon. You will have to be quick on your toes, make fast decisions and expect to come up against a lot of fierce competition. Fast-track businesses tend to exploit technology, fads and changes in consumer interests. A slow-track business will earn you money less quickly, but may have more long-term growth, with less immediate competition. Traditional high street businesses tend to be in the slow track. Which type do you think would fit in best with your personality and the skills and knowledge that you have?
2. Do you want to make things or to offer a service to others? Service businesses are generally cheaper to set up than manufacturing businesses.
3. Do you want to sell a lot of a lower-cost product to a larger market or a higher-cost product to a smaller market?

4. Do you want to be involved in an original business concept and idea? There are few of these around.

5. Do you want to be involved in a series of 'fad' businesses where you exploit consumer interest for perhaps six months or a year and then bail out when you spot another business opportunity to go into? Businesses that take advantage of an event or season (such as Christmas) fall into this category. Do you always want to be on the look-out for the unusual and the unique or do you want a more stable lifestyle?

6. Do you want to take an existing idea and do something different with it, so that in effect you create a new product or service?

7. Do you want to set up and run a traditional-style business, but do so in a different way that will make you stand out?

8. Do you like getting your hands dirty or do you prefer to be a paperworker?

9. Do you want to run just a 'day-to-day' business which earns you a living, but isn't going to set the world alight; do you want a global and wide ranging business empire like Richard Branson's or do you want something in-between?

10. Do you want a business that you can build up and then sell on, or do you want a business that you can keep in the family, building up a dynasty?

11. Do you want a business that can be developed in many directions or one that focuses solely on one area that you feel comfortable with?

How you answer such questions will depend upon your personality, your views of the future, your existing skills and the kind of things that you are interested in. If you are straight out of school or have little business experience, it's sensible to keep things as simple as possible. You will be learning many things at once, so don't overload yourself by taking on more than you can cope with.

Can you develop the idea?

Theoretically you can develop every business; however, it's easier to do this with some rather than others. These are some of the characteristics of business ideas that can be developed.

You must be able to repeat what you are doing time and time again. Businesses that depend on a one-off service or product, while they can earn you a good living, require a lot of your personal time and involve you in having to almost 're-invent' the wheel each time you sell to a new client or customer.

The business shouldn't depend solely on your efforts to make money and expand. For example, if you make rocking horses, but do so in a style that only you can produce, then your income will depend solely on how many horses *you* can make. This will limit what you can earn and how your business can develop.

You must either be able to expand it by sticking with the same idea but taking on ever more outlets for instance, or by using your original idea as a springboard to move you into other related areas. Look at Richard Branson. He started in the music business before moving into airlines, radio and condoms.

Businesses you should avoid

As with anything, to be most effective you should try to play to your strengths and away from your weaknesses, which you should have identified having worked through the previous chapter. Therefore you should avoid businesses that require:

- *Those needing a lot of experience*. With many businesses if you don't have the right experience you will not do a good job. This results in your not being paid because you haven't been able to do what you said you'd do or produced something that is not up to standard; taking so long to do the job that it isn't worth your while; or not being able to convince anyone that you can do the job in the first place.
- *Those needing a lot of skill*. As with experience, skill takes time to acquire and if you haven't got it you will suffer the

same problems as above. So avoid business ideas that require a high degree of skill unless you already possess it, can acquire it quickly or are able to team up with or buy in the skill from someone else.

- *Those needing a lot of finance*. As a general rule the more equipment and people you need to start a business up the more money you will require to finance it initially, and also probably to keep it going. If you are young and without a background in business, it's likely that you won't have the money yourself or be able to persuade others to lend it to you.

- *Slow-paying businesses*. With some businesses, even if you have sold something, you won't be paid immediately, especially when you are selling to other businesses. You will be expected to send in an invoice for your money and then wait 30, 60 or 90 days. Some types of business have traditionally long credit periods. You will have to make sure that you can survive while you are waiting for money to come in, so this also might require you to have a good initial financial cushion.

- *Those requiring you to pay for materials immediately*. On the other hand, there are businesses where you are expected to pay for goods or services immediately, which is the case with many types of trading. If your business idea requires this, you must make sure that you can cope with this payment out while waiting for payment in. You will have a double problem if you are also waiting a long time to be paid (see above).

Other opportunities

Whatever business you choose, you don't have to be stuck in a rut because being in one area of business doesn't mean you can't look for opportunities elsewhere. Indeed, a business can't survive in the long term with only one product or service aimed at one market alone. It must have strength in depth for long-term survival. Consequently, the best entrepreneurs don't pigeon-hole themselves into thinking that they can be or are just one thing. They take the view that they're in business to make money and what they do is just the vehicle for doing that at the moment. If you take the same view, you will start to see the world in a new light.

With this attitude, if you are running a catering business you would not think of yourself as a caterer, but as someone who was just making money from catering right now. When the time is right there may be another way to make money. Consider the example of Virgin. They started off as a record company, but have now branched out into the likes of condoms and, most spectacularly, an airline company. Similarly, Rentokil once contented itself with exterminating vermin. Now it does all manner of unconnected business.

Think this way and you will always be on the look out for opportunities that not only allow you to develop your existing business, but also let you move into other areas. And the more you look for opportunities the more you will find.

How to look for opportunities

- Take a notebook with you wherever you go and get into the habit of writing down any business ideas or thoughts immediately they come to you. Use a dictaphone or tape recorder if you have one to record your thoughts.
- Talk to people about what they do and ask them if they could see ways of doing it better, faster or more easily. This may indicate a business opportunity. Ask them also about the products and services that they use. What is wrong with them and how could they be improved?
- As a young entrepreneur you possess one particular advantage that older business people do not – you are far more in touch with other young people and what they are doing. This can reveal all sorts of potential markets, especially as many new trends originate here. Therefore, talk to your friends and ask them for their thoughts. What products would they like to have, what services would they like to be able to use.
- Don't just ask others for their impressions: think about

what products and services you buy and what happens to you in everyday life. This might indicate a business opportunity. What have you tried to buy and found wasn't available? What service would you have liked, but then found that it didn't exist?

- How are people spending their money these days? Where are they moving to live? What services are they demanding? Look for the trends.
- Look at existing businesses. How can you adapt their core idea to make it more interesting and marketable?
- Read as many different newspapers (two to three good daily papers, two to three tabloids and two Sunday papers), magazines and books as possible. Skim through them for potential business ideas. Analyse the advertisements that they carry. Do they suggest that people are becoming more interested in a particular subject, product, service or idea? Again, is there a way that this idea could be developed?
- What problems are people having at the moment? How can those problems be solved with a new product or service?
- What can you make safer, cheaper, cleaner, faster, brighter, lighter, heavier etc?
- What can you make or do at home that isn't done there normally, saving on overheads and giving you a price advantage?
- What can you make more quickly, conveniently or cheaply than others?
- What can you combine with an existing product or service to make a whole new product or service?
- Can you make something easier to package, store or transport?
- Can you make something less expensive to repair or replace?
- Can you make something more attractive or appealing to the market?
- Can you make something quieter or louder?

- Can you make or do something in less time or with less effort?
- Can you accessorise an existing product?
- Can you improve the distribution of an existing product or market it in a different way?

Is the idea right for you?

At some point you will have to call a halt on your search for a business idea and make a decision about what you are going to do. Remember, there is no perfect business idea. Many brilliant business ideas weren't brilliant when they started off, but the entrepreneurs made them so by the way they applied them and themselves.

So, you've thought of the business idea, but will it work for you, or does it have characteristics that make it difficult for you to put into action? Don't worry too much about choosing an idea that is not related to your previous experience: 50 per cent of people change their occupation when they set up on their own. It is more important to be enthusiastic; but you *must* think the idea through thoroughly beforehand. Now work your way through the following questions to assess the idea.

- What do others think of the idea?
- If it's a product, is it easy to make?
- Can you make it by yourself, or will you need others to help you?
- Can you easily get all the materials you need to make it?
- Can you afford to make it?
- Can you make the product to the right quality?
- Can you make the product to a consistent quality?
- Can you make it in sufficient quantities?
- Can you produce it at the right time and on time?
- Can you produce it often enough to keep up with demand?
- Can you produce it at a price that is acceptable?
- What do other people think of the product? Do they like it and think there is a market for it?
- Have people already expressed an interest in buying it?

- Will you be able to distribute your goods when you have made them, or will it be too expensive?
- Are there enough customers to make it worth doing?
- Is there an easy and affordable way of telling people about your product? Or will you find it difficult to promote your product or service to the market?
- Will you come up against stiff competition?
- Can you come up with some particular advantage that will make you different from your competitors?
- Will you need staff? If so, how many? Can you afford them right now? Are staff with the right skills available to you?
- How much and what type of space will you need to run your business? Can you find it where you want it and at the right price?
- Can you run your business from home?
- Can you run your business in the area where you live? If you can't, are you willing to move out of the area?
- What equipment will you need to run your business? Can you afford it? Can you make do with second-hand equipment?
- How many hours do you want to work each week? Will your business idea mean that you have to work more or less than this?
- How much money do you want to earn in a year? Will your business idea let you achieve this?
- What skills, knowledge and experience that you have now could you bring to your business idea?
- What special skills do you need to make this idea work? Do you have them? If you don't, can you find someone else with those skills, or learn them yourself in time?
- Would you feel comfortable running this type of business? Is it right for your character and personality?
- How much money do you need to make this business idea a success? Can you get that finance? (See Chapters 4 and 5.)
- How might this business idea fail? This is a question you

should keep asking yourself all through your entrepreneurial career.

The world of 'get rich quick'

If you have bought business magazines or read the business pages of the press, particularly of the more popular papers, you are bound to have come across advertisements for business opportunities. If you have already sent off for material on some of them, you will almost certainly be on the mailing list of others.

Many of these schemes and ideas aren't worth the paper they are written on, especially some of those involving multi-level marketing (or MLM). Generally, any ads that project immense and mouth-watering income opportunities within the space of months, or claim that you will make money very easily, have to be treated with suspicion and scepticism (two valuable personal commodities for any entrepreneur to acquire at an early stage). It's true that there are easy and hard ways to make money and that some people do make sizeable incomes quickly, but most of these schemes are for suckers and mugs. Most business people find that life isn't like this and that they need to work hard at their business for a minimum of five and more likely 10 or 15 years, rather than just a few months or even a year.

That said, not all of these opportunities should be dismissed out of hand. Some are based on sound business ideas that do work, which you can take on board yourself in their entirety or adapt to your particular situation.

The only real advice to be given is to treat everything with a degree of scepticism until you are satisfied. Downgrade all claims substantially. Be prepared to work hard to get any business opportunity off the ground, wherever the initial idea came from.

Plan of action

1. When you think of a profitable idea, take the first step to doing something about it immediately. You may decide very quickly that the idea 'doesn't have legs', which is

better than thinking that you'll get around to looking at the idea in a day or two: if you leave it longer, someone else will nick it.

2. What activities are you naturally drawn to? It doesn't matter what areas: sport, painting, animals etc. Write them down. Is there a business idea lurking here?

3. When you read stories in the press about business, can you see a pattern in your reading? Is there a type of business or story that always interests you more than others? If you aren't sure, monitor your reading over the next week or two, jotting down your thoughts and feelings on reading the papers.

4. Look for money-making ideas every day. Start at the beginning of the day and keep on through it. The more practice you have the better you will become at this.

5. Develop a couple of serious hobbies and see if these generate business ideas.

6. Start reading books on idea generation and pay particular attention to what they have to say about brainstorming.

4

How to Start Up

With an idea for a successful business under your belt, it's time to get down to the practicalities of actually getting your business up and running and earning money ... but not quite yet. There are still a number of issues to be sorted out.

Part time or full time?

If you are unemployed, have just finished school or college, or are working in a no-hope, low-paid, dead-end job, you may decide that you've nothing to lose and the sooner you get started in business the better it will be. That's fine, but for others the situation may not be quite so clear cut. For example, setting your business up on a part-time basis may be the right option if:

- you will need to raise extra capital before you can get the business really moving;
- you need the money from your main job to fund you while you get the business up and running;
- you aren't quite sure about the potential success of your idea and want to 'dip a toe in the water' to see if it works or not;
- you have family commitments that mean you can't go full time with the business just yet, but you still want to make a start;
- there are other pressures, perhaps from members of your family, that keep you from going full time.

In each case, setting up part time can be a sensible approach. However, if you are looking to do this while working for someone else there is one major difficulty – creating and managing the time to do both. If you try to begin in business this way you will need to find the time to plan and organise the start-up of your business, market yourself, make sales appointments, visit prospective customers and then actually do the work.

Understandably, this requires tremendous energy and effort and you will be putting heavy pressure on yourself which can reflect badly on the way you do your full-time job. If you are going to try to hold two jobs down at one time, you may be able to help the situation by:

- taking any unused holiday time to start up the business;
- rearranging your work hours so that you can go into work later or leave earlier;
- working night shifts, which will free up the day when you will need to be talking to clients, customers and suppliers;
- getting friends or relative to do some of the jobs for you while you are at work (for example, hunting down office equipment, getting stationery quotes or doing some of the background research);
- working on the business through your lunch hour or before you come into work;
- choosing a business which allows you to work in the evenings and at the weekends.

While these options mean that you make time available for yourself, this may all be wasted if you can't use these extra hours. For example, deciding that you can work on your business in the evening is no good if you need to make business calls to people at their place of work between nine and five.

If you intend to set up in the same or a similar business as you are already working in for an employer, you should check carefully to see if your contract of employment puts any restrictions on your doing business after you leave (for example, not within one year of leaving, or not within 50 miles of the employer's premises). Look carefully through your contract and staff handbook and any other such documentation. If it looks as though you will be restricted, you should seek legal advice about this as not all such restrictions are valid.

You should also take legal advice if you are thinking of trying to persuade any of your current employer's clients to place their work with your new business.

Starting a business at home

If you can, starting a business from your own house gives you a terrific initial advantage because it cuts out the cost of having to pay for expensive premises. It also reduces your ongoing costs and gives you the opportunity to test out your business idea without committing yourself to any significant long-term expense. What is more, it's terribly convenient, as you can stagger from bedroom to office in a matter of seconds. And if you have family commitments, it's a particularly good way of meeting them while still being able to work.

However, there are disadvantages. A home office may be *too* convenient, allowing you to take any opportunity to go and do something else around the house, not related to work. And though more and more people are now working from home (around 2.25 million are estimated to be doing so for at least part of their working week), there are still clients, customers and suppliers who don't take homeworkers or home-based businesses seriously.

Of course, not all businesses can be run from home either because they are unsuitable (you couldn't really sell health foods from your own home) or because they breach planning and building regulations or agreements with your building society or landlord.

Can you legally work from home?
Many houses and nearly all flats have conditions in their deeds which limit business activities. While some ban all business activity others prohibit only certain types of business. If you are in any doubt about what your deeds say you can and cannot do at the house or flat you should consult a solicitor.

What about tenancy agreements?
If you are a tenant, you should always check with the landlord what you can and cannot do. Some will have strong opinions

and refuse your permission to start up a business in their property, while others will adopt a more flexible approach.

Are you buying your home on a mortgage?

If you have a mortgage, whenever you set up a business at home you should tell the lender, though this is really only a matter of courtesy as there is unlikely to be any problem if it is a service business and using no more than a room or two. But if you intend to make substantial alterations to the house which could reduce the value of the property, in order to run the business, they are likely to have something to say.

Insurance

Your normal household insurance may be invalidated if you are running a business from home. Check the situation with your insurer and make sure that your business equipment is covered and that you have third-party insurance to cover visitors or workers in the house.

Do you need planning permission?

Planning permission is dealt with by the local authority, so if you are setting up a business you will need to contact them to see if you can run it from home. Special types of planning approval may be needed if you live in a listed building, a conservation area, an Area of Outstanding Natural Beauty or a national park. When deciding if you can run a business from home the planning authorities will consider:

1.   Will the main use of the house still be as a family home? If you are not using more than one room for your business, there should be few problems. Otherwise they may consider that you are changing the use of the house; you are also likely to run into problems with the mortgage lender if you are buying the house (see above).

2.   Will you be employing people on a regular basis? If so, permission may be needed, though if you are employing only one or two people this shouldn't be a problem.

3.   Are a lot of people going to be coming to your house on

business? If they are, you are likely to need planning permission since the neighbours probably won't take kindly to suppliers or salespeople ringing on your doorbell, parking delivery lorries all day long, and possibly blocking the road.

4. Will you need outside advertising to promote your business? If you are thinking of having signs or billboards outside, you will need permission. If you apply, it will most likely be refused.

5. Is your business going to create noise or fumes or work during unsocial hours? If it is, you will need permission. Think of those poor neighbours again.

6. Will you need to park a trade vehicle on your premises? If you do, you'll probably need planning permission.

If you are setting up a service-orientated business with most of your work being done over the phone or at the computer, there should little difficulty in setting up a business from home. Indeed, there is probably little point in contacting your local authority. However, if you are involved with making things, you are on thinner ice. You can of course set up without planning permission, but the council may order you to close down, in which case you will need to change all your stationery and a lot of your promotional effort will have been wasted.

Creating a home office

If you are going to run your business from home, you will need an office or at the very least an office-area to work from. If you live on your own, setting up an office will only involve pleasing yourself; however, if you live with your family, you will have to take a few things into consideration.

Choosing a suitable room
These are the main points to consider when deciding which room will be your office:

●   How affected is it going to be by noise and disturbance from the rest of the family? Ideally, a home office should be in the quietest part of the house.

- How much space will you need? Others in the family will try to force you into the second smallest room in the house, probably a spare bedroom. But is it big enough for the office equipment that you'll need?
- Will you need to see people in your office? If you do, it will have to be accessible and look efficient and businesslike. It is no good having your office up in the attic if visitors will be required to clamber up ladders and edge along narrow walkways.
- Does the office have enough daylight, ventilation and a temperature that is not too high in summer or too low in winter?

Setting up an alternative office

But what if you don't have, or can't negotiate with the rest of the family for, space for a dedicated home office? Well, there are a number of cost-effective solutions.

1. Create an office within another room such as the living room or dining room by having a bureau or small desk in one corner, from which you can work. For extra privacy you can use hessian, wood, or bamboo screens to partition off that part of the room.
2. Use the area under the stairs, perhaps putting up shelves and a foldaway desk or table. You will have to use your imagination to make the most of this option and you will need to pay careful attention to lighting.
3. If you have a garden, you could always put up a smart shed or conservatory, or convert an existing one, and use this as an office. However, while this may be fine in summer it could be very cold and damp in winter. You would also need to take a phone lead and an electricity supply out to it and make sure it is secure.
4. If you need more space, you could use the family caravan, or even a mobile home. Apart from holidays, these sit around doing nothing for the rest of the year; why not put them to good use?
5. Should your home not be suitable to work from, perhaps

you have a relative, friend or neighbour who has unused space they could make available to you.

6. You could share an office with someone else who wants to set up in business. You can offer mutual back-up when the other is out of the office, while sharing the costs of the premises. Remember that the person who signs the lease agreement will be the one responsible if the other does a 'runner', so it is safest for you both to sign the lease as joint tenants. You can either advertise in the local press for someone to share an office that you have or advertise for spare space in someone else's office.

7. If you don't need to spend very much time in an office and really need it as no more than a base, there is a variation to the above. You can approach existing businesses and negotiate an arrangement whereby you use the office for just the first hour or last hour of the day, or even before or after they have finished for the day. The advantage to the office owner is that they get an income out of their space when they are not using it fully, or at all. You can use this same approach if you are setting up a manufacturing business. There are companies out there who would be glad of the extra income provided by utilising their equipment's 'down time'.

8. You could use an office services company. These are businesses that will 'pretend' to be your office for you, answering the phone on your behalf, typing up letters and renting meeting rooms to you when you need them. You can find these advertising in the *Yellow Pages* under Business Centres.

Choosing commercial premises

Most young entrepreneurs won't be able to afford the cost of setting up in proper office or retail accommodation; however, if you can, consider the following points.

1. Do the premises need to have a certain 'look' that fits in with your business. If the building is in a slum district, you are not going to encourage well-heeled clients to visit you with their money.

2. Are the premises in the right location? There is no point setting up a retail outlet in an area where no one wants what you are selling. Similarly, people in the area might want what you are offering but don't know you are there because you are tucked down an alley. Also, are there enough people in the area to provide a market for you?

3. Are the premises the right size for what you need? Is there room for expansion or will you have to move very soon if the business takes off?

4. Are the premises being offered at the right price? Remember that premises are an ongoing cost that you will have to fund out of your sales.

5. How long will you have to commit yourself to taking premises for? At this moment in your business career, you won't be wanting to take on a long-term commitment.

You can find premises by looking through local newspapers, contacting estate agents and letting agents, the local authority for their lists of vacant industrial and commercial property, the local TEC or asking other business people.

Choosing office equipment

Now that you have a place to work you'll need equipment to fill it. You will probably be looking to do this as cheaply as possible, so the following points should help:

1. *The desk* doesn't need to be top of the range but bear these points in mind when looking:

    ● Make sure the underside of the desk is high enough to let you put your legs under comfortably.

    ● Look for a surface that is matt rather than shiny: the latter will reflect light into your eyes and can give you headaches.

    ● Make sure the desk is deep enough for what you want. If you intend to have a computer on it then it should be at least 75cm deep so that the computer screen is far enough away from your eyes not to cause problems.

- Watch out for sharp corners on the desk top: if the desk has these, you will inevitably end up walking into them.
- look for a desk with plenty of drawer space: Shallow ones for storing stationery, pens and rulers and deeper ones for files and directories.

You can make a very effective DIY desk by placing a flush-faced door on top of a pair of two-drawer filing cabinets placed a couple of feet apart. A panelled door can be used if a sheet of hardboard is put on top.

Whatever desk you have, position it at right angles to the window so you have an even spread of light falling on to your work and try to ensure it doesn't face a window. Not only will your eyes have to keep adjusting from outside brightness to the dimmer indoor lighting, but you will be distracted by what is going on outside. If you walk past office windows, look in: you will rarely find a desk facing outwards.

2. A good typist's *chair* can add greatly to your comfort when working in the office, so you should buy the best you can afford. Look for one that can be adjusted for height and gives good support to the back. For extra stability choose one that has a five-star base. The seat of the chair should be covered with a porous fabric so that any sweat in this delicate area is quickly absorbed. If you don't believe your bottom sweats, try sitting on a plastic chair during a hot summer's day!

3. A two- or preferably four-drawer *filing cabinet* is a minimum for your filing needs. There is no point buying these new, unless you are trying to impress clients, so look out for them at auction, office equipment sales, or offered second-hand in the local paper's classifieds.

4. Good office *lighting* is very important, not only for your eyesight, but also because trying to work under bad lighting is demoralising, which will affect your work rate and make you feel down. In the home, central pendant lights are normal, but these only light the centre of the room,

and your desk probably isn't there. So either move the light fitting, if you are DIY-minded, or simply run a longer length of electric cord from the central pendant and hang this over a hook screwed into the ceiling above the area you want lit. You should also have a desk light which can be angled, lowered or raised to focus a pool of light on what you are doing.

5. The *telephone* is an essential item of equipment. Though any machine will do at a pinch, for preference choose one that has at least a 20-number memory (it's surprising how many numbers you end up calling regularly; having to look them up on every occasion does waste a lot of time). Also look for a digital display that shows the number you have dialled; this prevents misdialling, again a waste of time. Phones that can be mounted on walls give you more desk space and keep the cord out of the way.

   If you work from home you may be able to make do with your domestic phone line to begin with (it will cut down on your start-up costs) but as soon as possible you should have another one put in. This ensures that your business is not interrupted by incoming or outgoing domestic calls. If you have a business line put in you will get a listing automatically in *Yellow Pages*.

   A mobile phone is probably not a vital piece of equipment when you are starting up, but it is fast becoming so, and may very well be right from the start if you are running the sort of business where you are out of your office for much of the time. It is also something of a status symbol, suggesting to others that you are a serious business person. When buying one, be very careful about what air-time package you sign up for as they can be very different in price. Shop around and choose the one that is most suitable for your needs.

6. Another essential item is an *answer machine*. For convenience the answer machine should display how many calls you have received. Make sure that the machine allows you to 'screen' calls by listening to them when you are there. Then, if you are busy you have the choice of answering or

not. This is an additional security feature for women who work by themselves. 'Remote interrogation' is also a very useful feature to have as this allows you to call your phone from another phone and listen to any messages that may be recorded on the answer machine.

You can also use BT's Call Return service very effectively with your answer machine. This gives you the phone number of the person who called you last, if you are on a new exchange, even if they didn't leave a message on the answer machine. It is available by dialling 1471 on your phone, and is a free service.

When you are not in the office, the answer machine is your secretary; therefore, its message should be professional, friendly and business-like because this is all part of the image you are trying to create for yourself.

If you are in a creative type of business, there is room for creativity with your answer machine message, but in general it is far better not to be gimmicky. The information to include in a message might be: the name of your company ('This is Compass Trading'), why the answer machine is on ('no one can take your call right now) and what the caller must do ('so please leave your message after the tone), what will happen after a message has been left ('and we will return your call as soon as possible') and any other information (alternatively telephone ...). Keep the message short as the caller is paying for the call and doesn't want to be paying out the pennies to be bored by your message.

If you are the only person in your business, it creates a better impression if you say 'we' rather than 'I' which does make the business sound small. Try to avoid including information that suggests you are out ('there's no one here right now'): burglars *do* phone up to see if there is anyone in.

If you are a gruff-voiced male, it is worth asking a female to tape the message as her softer voice will have a better quality to it and has the added advantage of suggesting that there are at least two people in the company.

If you do screen calls when you are working, don't be tempted to pick up the phone while the caller is talking unless it is someone you know well, or someone who calls very infrequently. If you do pick up the call midway through, the caller has a pretty good idea that you have been listening in. This will sow a seed of doubt next time they call. Are you there or are you not? Eventually, they may come to think that you are there the whole time, but just don't want to speak with them.

7. A *fax* is another essential piece of equipment, though you may be able to do without it for a few months when starting up. Faxes save a great deal of time and allow you to avoid the delay in sending information through the post. They are also a very good alternative to the phone when you just need to send a very brief message to someone. Most other businesses will expect you to have one.

8. For most start-up businesses, a *photocopier* is a non-essential and at first you should be able to make do with using a photocopier at the library, print shop or elsewhere in town.

9. When it comes to business, handwritten documents are right out because they look unprofessional, are often unclear and will harm your business-like image. You will therefore need at least a *typewriter* to prepare your business materials. Electric typewriters produce better quality documents than manual typewriters which leave an uneven impression on the paper when the character keys hit the paper.

10. However, far better than a typewriter is a *computer* with suitable software. There are very few businesses that positively have no use for one or aren't better off with one. This book is about entrepreneurship and not computers, so if you don't know anything about computers, go and learn. It's not difficult and the skill will always stand you in good stead if you want to be a successful business person. However, here are a few pointers on choosing the equipment you will need.

There are many different makes of computer and most of them will be suitable for your business, though making a final choice depends on what you want your computer to do. These are the four main uses:

● *Word processing*. Every business needs to prepare sales letters, business letters, invoices or other documents such as reports. Normally you will not need top-of-the-range word processing software, though useful features to have are a spell checker, mail merge and the ability to print envelopes. If word processing is all that you intend to use your computer for, you will not need a very powerful or fast machine. A 386 rather than a 486 machine will be enough, but it should have a large hard disk, say at least 80Mb, as space is used up very quickly, especially if you are using 'Windows'.

● *Accounts work*. Computers are very good at keeping your accounts. You can enter and change figures and it will automatically make all the calculations you need. It can produce profit and loss accounts and balance sheets. You can also do financial projections and cash flow forecasts that can easily be altered. For simple accounts you can use that 386 machine, but if you intend doing a lot of financial work you are better with a faster machine.

● *Database work*. If you are in the business of acquiring and holding a lot of information, such as names and addresses or customer information, a computer is the ideal piece of equipment because it can call up items of information quickly and easily. If you are regularly doing this type of work you should buy a fast and powerful machine.

● *Desktop publishing (DTP)*. This is a way of producing newsletters, brochures, booklets and other high quality documentation. DTP packages are much more flexible at doing this than even the best word processors. A good 486 or better computer is really needed for this, and a high quality printer. There are some attractively priced DTP software packages available; and if you have a creative streak, you could even try designing your own letterhead, business card and compliments slip, which will save you money compared to having it done professionally. Most businesses won't really need DTP though.

Once you have created a piece of work on the computer, you will need a *printer* to put it on to paper. Though there are a number you can choose from, for quality of the print, versatility and low initial cost look to either an ink-jet or bubble-jet printer, which can be had for a couple of hundred pounds. Laser printers are top-of-the-range models, so buy one if you can afford it, especially as their prices are coming down all the time. Unless you have them already and are using them as a stop-gap measure, avoid daisywheel and dot matrix printers as they can't produce the quality you want in your written materials.

Where to buy computer equipment

High street stores are convenient but their range of equipment may be limited as can be their sales expertise. Computer stores give good prices and offer more equipment, but are relatively few and far between and may not give much after-sales support. Computer dealers are generally more expensive, but can give good after-sales service, though they may seem too technical and rather unapproachable for the novice computer user.

The mail order suppliers advertising in national papers and computer magazines give very good prices and buying mail order is of course convenient, but you should make sure that you are buying from a reputable supplier. If you can, buy your equipment using a credit card. This should protect you if the supplier goes bust before they deliver. Some of the computer magazines in which they run ads provide indemnity schemes.

Computer equipment is also sold at auction for very good prices, but you have no guarantee that the equipment will work. Take an experienced computer user with you to test the machines. Buying second-hand can also give good bargains, but again there are no guarantees that the equipment will work. If you do buy second-hand, try out the computer and software before handing over money. Again, take along an experienced computer user with you.

Learn to touch-type

If you can't type yourself, you can always use the skills of mothers, sisters, brothers, girlfriends, boyfriends, relatives or friends. However, the most convenient and flexible answer is to learn to touch-type yourself. If you are committed to learning, it won't take you very long and there are plenty of books and even computer software around to help you. There are also evening classes if you'd prefer them. For the business person, touch-typing is far faster and more accurate than two-fingered 'pecking' at the keyboard, which is often inaccurate, slow and frustrating. And don't be arrogant enough to think that you won't bother to learn keyboard skills because you'll have a secretary to do it. At first you won't and even later, using computers is becoming so much a part of everyday business life that you may as well bite the bullet. In any case, typing a short letter yourself is far faster than dictating it to a secretary.

A source of help

If you do need to use computers or produce good quality documentation, but only occasionally, it is worth checking to see if you have a telecottage near you by contacting the Telecottage Association. Telecottages are places, often in rural areas, that have lots of computers, desktop publishing software, printers, scanners, photocopiers and faxes which the staff will train you to use for a modest sum.

Other equipment

These items certainly fall into the useful rather than essential category. They include an electronic calculator, helpful for doing accounts; a hand-held tape recorder or dictaphone, very convenient if you have a flash of inspiration while out walking or driving the car and want to make a note; a franking machine, time-saving and convenient if you do a lot of mailing, but an expensive toy if you don't send out much post; and a white-board or pinboard, on which you can put your daily goals, or stick notes to yourself or even use it for motivational purposes (see pages 138–39).

Do you need a business name?

Before you get going in business there is one more important thing that you have to do – decide what your business is going to be called. This is crucial as it helps to create the right image for your business.

You can of course trade under your own name, which is simple, convenient and doesn't need you to spend any time thinking up a name. It also reminds people who is the person in charge. Some people who use their own name also include their initials but this comes across as unfriendly: 'Peter Jones, Plumber' is more inviting than 'P J Jones, Plumber'.

But there are good reasons for not using your own name at all, but creating a proper name for your business. First, this makes your business appear larger than it is since there is no indication just how many people are involved in the business. If you use your own name, it suggests that you are a one-(wo)man band, or at least a very small company.

Second, a trading name makes your business seem more professional and business-like.

And third, if you have a name that is difficult to pronounce, to spell or gives off the wrong impression, people may be put off contacting you.

How to choose a business name

A well-chosen business name creates the right impression of your business, while a poor one does the opposite; so whatever name you choose, imagine yourself as a potential customer running their finger down a *Yellow Pages* listing. The only infor-mation they will have about your business is the name.

Try to think of a name that sounds good to the ear, but don't be tempted to use initials, for instance by reducing 'Sandra Jones Word Processing Services' to 'SJWPS'.

Long names catch the eye at first, but they can easily be forgotten. Make sure that any name you choose is appropriate to the type of business you are in.

You cannot use a name that is already in use, nor one that is too similar to another: you could not call yourself 'Rolls-Royce Clothing Company'. There are also a limited number of other words that generally cannot be used, for instance 'royal', 'bank' and 'insurance', or those which suggest a connection with central or local government.

Do you have the right address?

If you work from home, having the wrong address can reflect badly on your business, especially if your house is called something that is obviously residential, such as 'Chez Nous' or 'Mountain View'. If your house has both a name and a street number there is no problem with this as you can just drop the house name from your stationery.

However, if the house name is all there is to identify the property, you can always change it to something more appropriate. All you have to do is write to your local Royal Mail Customer Care Office, telling them that from a certain date your house will be known by its new name. The Customer Care Office will tell your local sorting office. You can call your property whatever you want, though it's sensible not to choose a name that is similar to a nearby property. The Customer Care Office should be able to tell you if there will be any likely problems.

Don't choose a property name that is too grand or claims to be your head or regional office, since if a client discovers the truth you will lose credibility. Unless you really have to, don't be tempted to use a Post Office (PO) Box number. Many people are suspicious of these thinking that you have something to hide and will just up and disappear overnight.

Plan of action

1. Write down the start date when you will do the first thing to set your business going.

2. What will this first thing be? Write it down.

3. Write down the start date when you will actually begin your trading.

4. Decide on a business name and whether you need to change your business address.

5. Contact *Livewire*. This is an organisation that offers a programme of business-orientated schemes and activities designed to help people aged between 16 and 25 be successful in the modern-day commercial world. Its main objectives include promoting awareness of 'enterprise' among young people; helping young people who want to start their own business; and helping young people who are already in business to develop. Livewire runs a number of business programmes such as the Livewire Business Planning Process which encourages sound business planning.

5

Money and Your Business

In this chapter we'll look at how much money you need to start your business and keep it going; how you can make the most of what money you do have; and how you can raise more money from other sources.

If you don't have a bulging bank account, a large number of businesses are immediately ruled out, and unless you can raise the money, you just have to live with that for the time being. But don't consider this as a problem.

How much money you will need to set up in business largely depends on the type of business you are setting up – a car dealer needs more money than a florist – but as a general rule service businesses tend to require less capital than manufacturing businesses. The reasons for this are simple. With a service business you are selling something you already possess: your skill and time. With a manufacturing business you have to buy the materials needed to make your product, the equipment with which to make it, and the means to store and distribute the product once you've made it.

There's nothing wrong with cutting your business teeth on smaller projects, moving on as cash comes in and your experience deepens. And if you fail in a small business, your commitments and debts probably won't be as great as they would be with a larger concern.

Your personal needs

Since you are in business to make money, it's important before you start to find out what money you will need to support yourself before your business gets going. It's a mistake to think that you will start earning an income from your entrepreneurial activity right away; indeed, it may be two or three months at a minimum before you do, and it could even be six months or more before you get paid. So you need to find out what your living expenses will be until then. Run through the checklist below to find out what they will be.

	Monthly amount	Six-monthly amount
Food		
Rent/mortgage		
Council tax		
Telephone		
Electricity		
Gas		
House insurance		
Travel/petrol		
Car insurance		
Car tax		
Car maintenance		
Medical insurance		
Personal expenses (toiletries, haircuts)		
Leisure		
Clothes		
Child care		
Household equipment		
Newspapers, trade journal		
Total		

That's probably quite a lot of money, but you can reduce it by careful planning.

Cutting down on your personal needs

Unpleasant though it may be, cutting back on your personal spending will give your business a better chance of succeeding, because it will allow you either to collect together more money which you can use as start-up capital or on-going working capital for your business, or to keep going just that little bit longer when your business isn't yet earning money. There are a number of ways in which you can cut down on your spending.

- Buy cheaper food. Shop around and visit markets and high street shops rather than supermarkets for better deals. Go just before closing time when you will often pick up bargains.
- Use cheaper transport. Buy, borrow or rent a bike. This is not only a cheap form of transport but one that keeps you healthy and fit. Walk to places if you can. This may be slower, but it's even cheaper than a bike and gives you time to think about your business. Flashes of inspiration often occur when walking. Also use off-peak public transport. If you are a car owner take it in turns to share vehicles with others and cut down on the number of trips you make by planning ahead so your shopping and other needs are catered for by fewer trips.
- Cut down on socialising and entertainment. This doesn't mean becoming a hermit, but if you do go out to the pub, have one drink less; if you go out to a restaurant, don't have the starter; instead of going to the cinema, rent a video. And start using free types of entertainment such as art galleries, museums, countryside walks, exhibitions and more. Console yourself that you'll be able to do all of these things really well when your business is succeeding.
- Don't buy books unless they are used constantly, but use the local library. Buy magazines only if you need them for research.
- If you have the skills, mend and repair things yourself rather than calling in repairmen.
- If you need household goods, buy cheap ones (if quality

isn't too important), second-hand or swap one piece of equipment for another with someone else.

- Don't go to the latest (and most expensive) hair salon; ask a friend with hairdressing experience to do the job for you. But make sure they can do a reasonable job. As a serious business person you need to look smart and not be wandering around with a pudding-basin haircut.
- Turn becoming a temporary miser into a game. Whenever you think you need to spend some money, think to yourself, 'Do I have to spend this at all?' and 'If I do need to spend money, do I need to spend this much?'
- Keep a record of how much you are (not) spending and revise it regularly. This is the score card of your financial success because as savings rise you will be moving nearer and nearer towards what you need as start-up capital.
- Set weekly budgets for your personal needs. Commit yourself to staying within them and be hard on yourself if you fail. This is all good training for your business career where the same sort of constraints will be imposed on you. However, be aware that accidents and the unexpected do happen which might cause you to break your budget through no fault of your own.
- Try to save a little money each week and put it away in an interest-earning account.
- Don't undertake any new commitments (such as hire-purchase agreements etc) unless you have to.
- If people owe you money, try and pull it in before you start your business; the same goes for any back pay you may be due.

How much finance does your business need?

If you aren't careful, even with smaller and less financially thirsty businesses, you can still find your start-up costs shooting towards the moon. Whatever business you are in, meticulous financial planning is important. One of the most common reasons for business failure is under-capitalisation: not having enough money to run the business.

Your start-up money

One of your first steps is to decide exactly what equipment, materials and outside help you need to begin your business. Below is a checklist that contains many of the items required to set up a service-orientated business or the office of a manufacturing business. Obviously, it can't cover the needs of every kind of manufacturing operation so add your own essential items to the list.

	Priority?	Cost new	Cost second-hand	Purchase date
Desk(s)	Y/N			
Chair(s)	Y/N			
Filing cabinet(s)	Y/N			
Filing system	Y/N			
Shelving	Y/N			
Desk light	Y/N			
Overhead light	Y/N			
Other furnishings	Y/N			
Franking machine	Y/N			
Pinboards	Y/N			
Reference books	Y/N			
Letterheads	Y/N			
Business cards	Y/N			
Compliment slips	Y/N			
Envelopes	Y/N			
Other stationery	Y/N			
Postage	Y/N			
Office diary and phone book	Y/N			

	Priority?	Cost new	Cost second-hand	Purchase date
Promotional brochures	Y/N			
Advertising costs	Y/N			
Other promotional costs	Y/N			
Accountancy fees	Y/N			
Solicitors' fees	Y/N			
Other fees	Y/N			
Insurance	Y/N			
Room heater	Y/N			
Decoration materials	Y/N			
Computer	Y/N			
Software	Y/N			
Printer	Y/N			
Computer supplies	Y/N			
Computer accessories	Y/N			
Fax	Y/N			
Modem	Y/N			
Phone	Y/N			
Mobile phone	Y/N			
Answer machine	Y/N			
Photocopier	Y/N			
Scanner	Y/N			
Typewriter	Y/N			
Equipment repair contracts	Y/N			
Research materials	Y/N			

	Priority?	Cost new	Cost second-hand	Purchase date
Car/van	Y/N			
Car/van insurance	Y/N			
Car/van road tax	Y/N			
Incidental travel expenses	Y/N			
Specialised equipment	Y/N			
Clothing	Y/N			
Other	Y/N			
TOTAL				

Having made your own list, consult catalogues, visit shops and stores and obtain quotes for each item. This will give an idea of how much setting up new and from scratch will cost. Don't forget to add VAT on items, if it is not included. Be prepared to overestimate the true costs. It is better to be on the high side rather than come up with an underestimate.

Next, go down the list again and decide which items you already have or can borrow. As this makes these effectively free, take them out of your financial checklist. If you do borrow equipment, be careful about becoming reliant on items that the lender might suddenly want back, leaving you in the lurch.

If your business doesn't need spanking new equipment, then don't buy it. Whenever you buy anything new, when it leaves the showroom, it loses perhaps a third or even half of its value. So why bother with new? You are much more sensible to spend your money on good and workable second-hand equipment and using the difference in price to promote your business.

Office furniture is generally hideously expensive and you can make major savings here, especially if you are working from home, where clients and customers are unlikely to see it. So go down the list again and identify those items which don't need to be new (very few of them do need to be) and can be second-hand.

You will find second-hand office equipment offered for sale in local newspapers, at local auctions or at secondhand equipment stores (look in *Yellow Pages*). Call up, find out prices, then add 10–15 per cent in case you can't get them at these bargain prices when you do come to buy. Adding all these together should give you a realistic estimate of what it would cost to set up, but add on another 20 per cent just to be on the safe side.

Wow, it's that much! If you have the cash, you've no problem; you simply make a decision about whether you wish to spend it in this way. But what if you don't have that amount of money? Don't despair immediately. There are a couple of options.

First, choose another business idea which doesn't need so much money to start up; this may not involve coming up with another idea at all but simply modifying your original idea.

Second, go down the above list again and decide which items are an essential for your business now and which you can put off buying or getting for one month, three months or six months. If you can stagger your purchases in this way, you won't need so much start-up capital. Always be honest with yourself when it comes to buying additional, more expensive, or more up-to-date equipment. Always ask 'Do I really need this?' Do you really need a faster and more powerful computer, or will the one you have now do for another six months? Do you really need a mobile phone, or are you buying it just to look cool?

If your suppliers are offering any special bargains or offers, take advantage of them, but don't do this if it means you are going to be left holding and storing materials that you won't need for ages. Therefore, when faced with the tempting offer of buying 100 pens or 10 reams of paper hold on to your pennies. It is better to pay more for each individual item now and keep the rest of your money in the bank, ready to be used elsewhere in your business.

And third, if you still need every item on the list then you can look for ways to raise the finance to buy them. There are a number of financial sources which you can contact.

Taking out a bank loan

Obtaining a loan can be a problem if you are young, don't have a track record in business, or don't have the business skills that lenders are demanding.

Choosing the right bank

If you need a business account it should probably be one of your first ports of call. You will already probably have a personal account and you may well want to stay with your current bank for your business banking. But you may want to shop around. If you do, the following points should help.

First, do some background research by reading the literature that the banks themselves put out. What impressions do you get? Which of them makes you feel the most comfortable? Is there a particular aspect they are promoting which seems to fit in with what you are doing? Are there any financial incentives which might induce you at the moment to go with one bank rather than another, for example offering free banking for a year? Though the banks hope that in part your laziness (as well as their service) will keep you with them after 12 months, there is no reason why you shouldn't take advantage of their kind offer and then leave in 12 months. If there is a reason why you can't do this, you should think very carefully about taking them up on the offer in the first place.

Ask other business people who they bank with. What service have they received from that bank and particular branches. What are the personnel like with whom they have had dealings? Are they helpful and well informed or obstructive and even ignorant of what their bank has to offer? Even though banks are run pretty much from the top down, the personal element is still important; and having a good relationship with the staff, particularly the manager, is important. Banking, whatever you might think at times, is still operated and run by humans, who have emotions, sensibilities and feelings. If you are involved in a marginal decision, you are more likely to receive help from a manager with whom you can laugh, than one who doesn't get on well with you.

Alternatively, ask your accountant for advice (you will need one if you are going into business). He is dealing with bank managers regularly and is obtaining feed back from his own clients on the particular characteristics of local managers and branches.

Be serious in your hunt for a suitable bank. Visit all branches in your area and book an appointment, preferably with the manager. If you can't see the manager quickly, be prepared to wait until you can. Unless you are in a tearing hurry, don't see an assistant or even a business adviser, who has probably had little business experience and may well try to 'come over all superior' when they know your age and lack of business experience.

When you go to meet the manager you should dress smartly. You don't need a formal three-piece suit, but a jacket and tie is a sensible choice. If you turn up in jeans, the manager may immediately question your seriousness and commitment to your business. It may seem false to do this, but you are a player in the game, and the bank manager will want to see that you at least know the rules. You will find more about creating the right business image for yourself in Chapter 7.

Outline your business venture and your experience and ask how the bank would go about dealing with your account. Where do they think the problems will lie and what things should you look out for?

Borrowing money from the bank

If you are seeking funding, you should make this clear when you make the appointment so that enough time is set aside to discuss it. Take your business plan (see below, pages 90–93) with as much documentation as you can lay your hands on, though don't go over the top. Make sure that everything is prepared so that you can easily move from one document to another. If charts and plans will help your case, take these with you and use them. Have a rehearsal before going so that you present slickly, or at least competently.

Be prepared to have your ideas and plan shot at. However,

your self-assessment and all the work you have put in on your sturdy and watertight business plan should have highlighted the weaknesses in your venture and forced you to think about countering them.

If your idea is likely to be unfamiliar to the manager, take additional background material with you and be ready to fill in with information that will paint a clearer picture of the industry. Reassure the manager by outlining any interest there has been in this idea from major companies, whose names he knows, and which can act as a comfort blanket.

The bank agrees to a loan

The smaller the loan you are looking for, the less difficulty you should have, and if you are asking for anything less than £5,000 the manager should be able to handle the transaction without having to refer it to higher levels in the bank.

If and when you get agreement from the manager, don't rush over with hugs and kisses, but play it a little cool. Thank the manager for the meeting which you think has been highly productive and rewarding, but say that there is quite a lot to think through in terms of the detail of the deal (this will definitely be the case if you are offering your house as security, or if different rates of interest apply), and that you would like a few days to think the proposition over and also to look at a couple of other options. In a subtle fashion you are telling the manager that you are shopping around for the best deal. You may know already that this is the only deal on offer, but the manager doesn't.

The Loan Guarantee Scheme

The manager will be looking to secure the loan if he can. This reassures him that he can get 'his' money back if you default on payments. However, the chances are that you won't be able to offer him any security, either because you have no property, or because it is already mortgaged up to the hilt. If you have no security the bank may ask you to use the government-backed Loan Guarantee Scheme.

Under the scheme the Department of Trade and Industry (DTI) guarantees part of the loan a bank may make to a small business. For a new business, the DTI will guarantee 70 per cent of the loan. You will be expected to borrow a minimum of £5,000 and a maximum of £100,000. You can have several guaranteed loans at the same time as long as they do not exceed the maximum ceiling. However, the bank will not put up your scheme to the DTI if it considers you have only modest chances of success.

Sole traders, partnerships, franchisees, limited companies and co-operatives are all eligible for the scheme, as are most types of business, though there are exceptions. To qualify you must already have applied to the bank for a loan and been turned down on the grounds that you did not have sufficient security.

When you take out a guaranteed loan you will be expected to produce quarterly management and cash-flow reports and also projected figures.

This scheme is useful, but can be expensive as you will have to pay quarterly premiums on top of the loan repayments. There is also the time involved in actually producing the documentation that the DTI demands. To find out more, contact your bank, who will be able to tell you more. You can also contact the DTI Loan Guarantee Scheme direct.

Developing your banking relationship

Above all, remember that the manager must always feel comfortable doing business with you, so you should stay in touch with him regularly and advise him of any problems that may be coming up. He may temporarily be able to change the terms of your loan and improve matters for you.

Even if you have a good relationship with your bank, still check your bank charges regularly, as the bank will try it on from time to time as it is a business seeking profits. If you think you have been unfairly treated, kick up a fuss. The last thing the manager will want is to be drawn into a long and expensive correspondence and discussion about a letter for which you have been charged £15 if it is going to cost the bank of couple of hundred pounds of the manager's time.

One final point to remember: no matter how well you get on with one manager at one branch, don't be tempted to put all your financial eggs into one basket. This will give the lender far too much control over what you can and cannot do.

Thirteen ways to improve your credit rating

Credit makes the world go around, or so it seems, particularly if you can't get it; and more and more modern services, from mobile phone air-time to on-line computer information services require you to have it. But, if you have left college in debt, as many students have, or have had a few bad financial experiences, you may have problems obtaining loans. In that case, there are a few steps that you can take to improve your credit rating and therefore your chances of obtaining a loan.

1. Details of your financial history are held by credit reference agencies and it is to them that lenders will turn when you apply for credit. If lenders do not like what they see, such as defaulting on loans or late payments, they will refuse you credit. This information can stretch back up to six years. You will probably be aware of any 'little difficulties' that are likely to be here, but your first move should be to check anyway. The three main agencies are listed in Chapter 10.

2. Once you have obtained your details from the credit reference agencies, this will reveal what information about you potential lenders will see. If it's wrong, you can have it removed or altered. You can't amend information that's correct; however, you can put it in some kind of perspective by attaching an explanatory comment of up to 200 words to your reference. This is your chance to put your side of the story, so you should mention the circumstances which put you in the situation, for example personal or family illness, redundancy or a major customer going bust.

3. In some cases, lenders will refuse credit, not because of your financial history, but someone else's, such as an ex-spouse or your adult child still living at home. If this is the case, write to the agencies and explain to them that though you may live at the same address you have no financial connection with them.

4. If possible, clear outstanding debts on your credit reference as new credit is unlikely if debts or judgements are outstanding.

5. When you have cleared your debts, write to the credit reference agencies and tell them that you want this recorded on your reference.

6. When you clear any county court judgements that may be outstanding against you, write to the court and ask for a certificate of discharge. This demonstrates that you have paid the debt and you can show it to potential lenders. Some companies claim they can remove county court judgements for a fee. Before using them, check with their local Trading Standards Office that there are no complaints against them and preferably seek a recommendation from someone who has used them successfully.

So far we have dealt with your credit history, but now it's time to start improving your 'credit present'. Besides containing bad information, credit references also hold the good news about your financial background, such as when you took and paid back loans on time. The next stage in your creditworthiness campaign is therefore to put more of this 'white' information on your reference.

7. If your business is strengthening, your bank account healthy, or personal circumstances changing for the better, tell lenders this when you make your application. Even include a personal budget plan showing income (with proof) and regular outgoings so that you are providing lenders with positive information. Lenders may use a credit reference agency as the main source of information about you, but lending is discretionary so they can take other information into consideration.

8. If you are turned down by a lender, apply elsewhere. Not all lenders use the same criteria for assessing loan applications.

9. Many lenders are anonymous organisations making thousands of lending decisions every day. To them you are literally just a name and number. Therefore, look to those who

can put a face to your name: your existing bank and building society. Build bridges with them by arranging an appointment and ask their advice about how you can climb back on to the straight and narrow. Ask what you would have to do to get a small loan, say of £300 or £500, from them. Find out such things as how much you have to keep accounts in credit by, and how long you have to do that before they will examine your situation. Take heed of their words.

10. Apply for a loan from them, small and for a short period. The loan doesn't have to be for anything specific; indeed, you could immediately put it into an interest-bearing account, preferably one that allows you access every month before payment is due on your loan. Shop around for the best deal, but don't put the money with the bank or building society you've just borrowed it from. You might consider splitting the money, paying in different amounts over a few weeks. This makes it look as though the money isn't just from one source. By doing this you are effectively paying (the interest payment difference between the savings account and the loan account) to improve your credit reference. Now all you have to do is keep up the loan payments. You may like to pay off the loan a month or two early. You can then take out another larger loan, though still a relatively small amount, and do the same thing. (By now you should be realising that improving your credit worthiness can be a slow process.)

11. Offer to take out payment insurance when you apply for a loan. The lender may then feel that they have a degree of security in the event of your future ill health, or business difficulties.

12. Try to establish a credit account with a local supplier, preferably one you have dealt with regularly and sensibly. Do this and you may at a later date be able to ask your supplier if you can use him or her as a credit reference; not everyone uses the standard credit reference agencies.

13. Look for more sympathetic sources of loans, which may employ less strict criteria than financial institutions. These

might include business loans to minority or special interest groups, or those in particular localities. Another source are credit unions, which are like community banks. They lend funds against money you have saved with them. Hire-purchase may also be easier to obtain than standard credit if you need goods. But don't be tempted to take loans from less scrupulous lenders who are unlikely to take a lenient attitude if you default on a loan.

When it comes to improving your credit rating there are no guarantees that these suggestions will be successful but you are taking positive steps to rectify the situation. However, don't expect miracles; those who have had their homes repossessed or been made bankrupt will find the road to credit up an uphill one. If you can't get credit, look on the bright side and view trading in cash as a blessing in disguise offering you no chance of getting into debt.

Other ways to finance your business

1. In recent years young entrepreneurs have been taken far more seriously, so much so that a number of organisations have been set up either to provide entrepreneurs with funding or to help them find it. The schemes are varied and wide ranging, which means that it is easiest and best to contact each organisation direct to find out what they offer. Your local TEC will be able to tell you what is on offer. However, one of your first contact points should be the Prince's Youth Business Trust which offers finance and support to entrepreneurs under the age of 30 (31 if they are disabled). Livewire also has a Business Start Up Award which provides more than £175,000 in cash and kind to young business managers in their first year of trading.

2. Business start-up grants should be very high on your list of financing options. They will provide you with a weekly income while you are getting your business up and running. Some of these grants will require you to have a certain amount of capital to qualify and may well expect

you to attend training courses before giving you funds. Consult your local TEC or LEC.

3. Find out if there is a Local Investment Networking Company in your area. LINCs try to put businesses looking for funds in touch with investors who have money available. Often the amount of funding on offer is quite large. A growing number of Enterprise Agencies are running LINCs. Check with your local TEC.

4. If you live in the countryside, you could apply to the Rural Development Commission for funding. The RDC sometimes has loans for buildings, plant and equipment available to small businesses.

5. Try the EC, which has many grant schemes available, particularly if you are in certain areas of the UK. Your local Enterprise Agency or Development Agency should be able to tell you what's on offer. Companies have been set up to advise on the availability of grants. They may or may not be able to find you suitable sources of funds, though if you can, try to secure a no success, no fee agreement. The publication *Grants for Business* provides information on a range of financial sources.

6. Contact your local authority and see if they have any loans or grants available. Their business development officer is probably the person to talk with first.

7. Venture capital companies may be an option for you, but only if you are looking for pretty substantial funding. As a first point of call, you should contact the British Venture Capital Association who produce a free annual directory of members who are willing to provide venture capital. If they are to give you funds, you will have to have your business plan and your whole business venture very well thought out and formulated.

8. Can you obtain funding from private investors? There are solicitors, accountants, stockbrokers, possibly in your local town, who could be searching for companies in which they could put funds, either on their own behalf or on behalf of their clients. Again, you will have to have a good

business plan if you are to convince them that you are a worthwhile risk.

9. Check the small ads of your local newspapers and also business publications for people who are offering investment funding. These 'business angels' will need convincing of the quality of your business venture so you should have your business plan ready.

10. The Capital Exchange provides a forum to people who either have funds to offer or are looking for funding. It works in a similar way to the Stock Exchange but deals with smaller companies. Businesses that want funds pay a joining fee to become Capital Exchange members. For this they will receive regular entries in the *Capital Exchange Gazette* which is distributed to those who have funds for offer.

11. If you have experience in the armed forces then you may qualify for an interest-free loan from the Royal British Legion.

12. Take on a business partner who can inject funds into your business. You will have to negotiate with them about what exactly they are going to get out of the relationship and how much involvement they will have in the day-to-day running of the business. If they put in a large amount of money, they may well try to take control of the business either if they see that things are going well (they want everything for themselves) or if they are going badly (they want to try and save the business).

13. How about issuing shares in your business? Large companies do so, why not you? You won't be able to offer them on the London Stock Exchange, but you could always create ten £100 shares which you sell to investors. You will have to tell people what they receive from being shareholders, in terms of financial reward or special treatment. Again, you will need to draw up a suitable agreement.

Issuing shares is in one sense better than taking on a business partner because, by carefully setting up the arrangement, you will deny the shareholder any ability to influence your business decisions. However, you may well have difficulty selling the shares because it can seem an unusual idea to many people.

One refinement of issuing shares is to incorporate a 'share buy-back' option. This simply states that at a later, specified date, you will buy the shares back from them. This allows you to raise funds in the meantime, while not having to relinquish control of the company.

14. If your business looks as though it is going places, you could always let someone pay you to create their job! This might appeal to another young person, perhaps currently unemployed, who has some funds available either themselves or can raise funds elsewhere. You would have to convince them of the potential success of your business, or that they would gain valuable experience in the short term which they could then take on to other companies. From their point of view this would be very valuable in helping them to overcome the frequently encountered problem of 'sorry you've no experience so you can't have a job.' They could pay you weekly or monthly if you really just wanted no more than day-to-day working finance, or in one lump sum if you need a larger sum of money upfront.

15. Dip into your savings, but don't go mad. If you can, always leave something in the kitty for emergencies. When you are beginning in business the unexpected inevitably happens so allow for it and try to have some cash available to cover the 'disaster'.

16. Cash in any shares, stocks or premium bonds you have. When selling these, you should remember to allow for the dealing costs you will incur. Also check out the standing of the share with a broker. The last thing you want to do is sell a share whose price is about to go through the roof.

17. Do you have any life assurance policies that you could borrow against or cash in? This is really only viable if your policy is near to maturity. Cashing in a young policy, one that you have taken out recently, will be like throwing money down the drain as you will probably end up with

very little, only just covering the set-up charges. You should contact your insurance company to discuss the situation. Find out what the difference is in the value of the policy if you cash it in now or wait until it matures.

18. Sell unwanted or surplus items. It's surprising what you can find in the attic, wardrobes, garage and shed. Find buyers by asking friends and family, using small ads in the local paper, or car-boot sales. Unless you have a lot of assets, selling your belongings is probably only going to raise a small amount.

19. If you run a reasonably good car, why not trade down temporarily to a smaller, less powerful model? This will not only give you a cash sum in your hand but also lower your monthly payments on petrol, insurance and servicing.

20. If you need to raise larger sums consider borrowing against your house or flat, if you own one. It can be a very cost-effective means of raising finance. However, you will obviously need to be committed to your business venture if you take this route since you could lose the property. Contact your building society or bank and talk to them about the possibilities.

21. Back to the bank. Can they offer you an overdraft? If they can, this will cover your financial needs in the short term. Make sure you understand this, because using an overdraft to borrow money for longer periods can be very expensive, not to say dangerous. Overdrafts can be withdrawn by the bank without notice. Always use the most appropriate means of financing if you are borrowing money. Talk with your accountant about what type of finance to use. The cheapest source of finance may not always be the best.

22. Pension schemes aren't generally a top priority when you're young, but if you have one then you may be able to borrow against it. A pensions adviser or your accountant should be able to give you advice on the benefits and disadvantages of doing so. There are likely to be financial penalties if you take this course of action.

23. Borrow from family, friends or relatives, but only take it if they can afford to lose the money. Taking your white-haired grandmother's life savings to finance your risky business venture, if it's all that stands between her and the street, is only for the most unscrupulous. If you borrow from family, don't take the money for granted but draw up an agreement with them, just as you would with any business transaction. The agreement should state the terms on which you have borrowed the money, how much you intend to pay back and when, and any other restrictions or conditions that may be attached to the loan. This will impress and help to reassure them and is all part of adopting an entrepreneurial attitude.

    You can better sell the idea to them if you have a sound and well-thought-out business plan and don't just go along cap in hand with a half-thought-out idea of what you want to do. You may also want to involve them in the business, for their moral support and also to increase your chances of obtaining the money from them.

24. If your wallet is full of plastic, you could do some very short-term financing with your credit cards. If you pay off the outstanding amount before the due date you will have had no cost credit. You obviously can't use this method of finance for longer-term needs as it would be too expensive.

25. Contact suppliers or potential suppliers and see if they will give you trade credit. If they can offer you a period during which you do not have to pay for the goods and services that you are using, you are improving your cash flow and effectively raising finance for yourself.

26. If you have any outstanding loans, can you renegotiate them so that they are more favourable to you? By extending your loans, though you will be paying out more in the long term, you will be reducing your current monthly outgoings. You should check out the implications and the costs of doing this with your accountant and the lender.

27. Could someone borrow on your behalf? If your credit rating isn't good, maybe a relative or friend will take out a

loan and then give you the money. Obviously, they will need to have a great deal of trust in you as they will have the legal responsibility of paying back the loan. Again, you should draw up an agreement with them and convince them of the value of their actions by showing them your business plan. They might demand some security from you.

28. Rather than tie your funds up in capital equipment you can always lease it. When you lease equipment it will have implications not only for your cash flow but also for your tax situation. You should discuss these matters with your accountant and also with the Finance and Leasing Association. When you lease equipment you never own it: it remains the property of the leasing company. An advantage of leasing is that you have up-to-date equipment and change to the latest model when renewing the lease.

29. If you need equipment, you can buy through hire-purchase. Though this is generally a rather expensive way to finance your business, it does allow you to obtain equipment and materials that you would not otherwise be able to afford. When you have made the last payment on the hire-purchase agreement, that item becomes yours.

30. If you have spare rooms or space in your house, why not take in a lodger? If you don't want to go to this extreme, but have a sizeable office, you may be able to rent out part of this, with your 'office mate' sharing your working and equipment facilities. There may be some health and safety legislation which affects you if you rent out office space, so check first with the Health and Safety Executive.

31. Can you rent out usage of your office equipment, such as the fax, copier or computer? You would need to market this facility by placing small ads in local publications. If you do this, you should be prepared for the frequent interruptions that will occur as you have to show people how to use the equipment and deal with the queries.

32. Try bartering your services by swapping your services or products for someone else's. For instance, you could pay

for a new computer or fax by offering to provide a certain number of hours' work, or a certain amount of your product in return.

Finding an accountant

One of your greatest allies in obtaining financial help and advice will be your accountant, so it is worth shopping around until you find a good one. Accountants can advise on most financial issues that will affect your business. These include what structure your business should have (sole trader status or limited company); the best sources of finance; how to cost your work; setting up bookkeeping systems; and drawing up a business plan. To find an accountant:

- Ask other people who are in business, or who have been, if they can recommend an accountant, but make sure that it is a recommendation. Just don't accept that if someone says they use 'old Joe Bloggs' that he is any good, they may just use him through habit.

- Look through the *Yellow Pages* and the *Thomson Directory*, contact local business organisations and the Institute of Chartered Accountants for lists of their local members.

- Now with a list of four of five accountants in your back pocket, visit each before you start in business and explain to each what you and your business are trying to do.

- Ask each what they can offer to your business and why they think they can be of help to you. In effect, you are interviewing the accountant; after all you are the customer.

- Ask for their initial reaction to your business idea. Are they positive, non-committal or uninterested. It would be good to have an accountant on board who was interested in what you are doing.

- Consider whether you can get on with this accountant. Do you feel they are being rather patronising towards you because of your age? Do you feel that they will be over-cautious, not giving you the encouragement that you need?

Writing a business plan

By now you have done a lot of thinking about your business, what you want out of it, what you are going to make or do and how you are going to do it. Now you need to formalise all of that by creating a business plan. This serves a number of purposes.

First, it lets you get things clear about your business by writing them down on paper. Second, once these thoughts and objectives are down on paper you now have a document that you can use to persuade others to give you financial help. And third, you have a document that you can regularly refer to so as to make sure that your business is going in the direction that you want it to.

This can only be a brief outline of what a business plan should be about and there are plenty of books around that expand on this topic. Your accountant will also be able to offer advice. However, there are a couple of sections to which you as a young business person should pay particular attention.

Your business plan, as well as providing you with a realistic framework for operating, may also point up potential weaknesses in your business. These are likely to be your lack of management experience and your ability to market and sell your product or service.

Therefore you should pay careful attention to how you overcome these shortcomings, either by obtaining the training and experience yourself or employing someone else to cover this area of inadequacy.

If you are going to use your business plan to impress a potential investor, you should write it in the third person (use the style of 'It is considered that . . .', rather than 'I consider that . . .'), have it typed up carefully and read it thoroughly twice to remove mistakes and then present it in a new, hard-backed folder.

What needs to be in your plan?

Every business plan divides into a number of sections. These are usually as follows:

Summary

- what is your business about?
- where are the markets that you are going after?
- what is the potential for your business?
- what profit do you expect to make?
- how much money do you need to set it up?
- what's in it for anyone who is lending you money?

This section needs to be just one or two pages long.

Past history

- when the business was set up
- how it has performed in the past (obviously if you are setting up a new business then you would leave out this section)

This section should be about one page long.

The management

- your previous employment, if any
- your previous business experience and achievements, if any
- the background of any other people working with you
- how you propose to deal with obvious weaknesses in the management; this will be a very important section if you are to convince others that you are going to create a viable business.

Take as many pages as you need to complete this section.

Your product or service

- a basic description of your product or service
- the unique advantages of your product or service
- an outline of the competition
- how you intend to develop your product or service in the future

Allow two pages for this section. Any particularly technical detail can be put in a separate section at the back of your business plan.

Marketing

- what is the current size of the market?
- how has the market grown in the past?
- how is it likely to grow in the future?
- why your business is aimed at this particular segment of the market
- who your likely customers are
- how many of them are there?
- who are your competitors and how are they likely to respond to your new business?
- how you are going to promote your business (see Chapter 6 for more on how to market your business)
- who will do the selling?
- what will be your sales pitch?
- how will you price your product or service?

This section will probably cover three to four pages in your business plan.

Operating details

- where will you be based (at home, high street, office, factory)?
- who will be your suppliers?
- what will your manufacturing facilities be like?
- what equipment will you need?

The length of this section will really depend on the type of business you are running. For service businesses this section will be shorter than for manufacturing businesses.

Financial situation

You will probably need help from your accountant, or business adviser, to complete this section of your business plan properly.

- a summary of the monthly profit and loss, monthly cash flow and balance sheet forecasts
- the monthly profit and loss forecast for the first two years
- a profit forecast for another three years

- the monthly cash flow forecast for two years
- the cash flow forecast for another three years
- a forecast balance sheet for the first two years
- the assumptions behind the forecasts
- the major risks and changes that might affect these forecasts

This section will take up two to three pages. Exact figures may be given in another section at the back of the plan.

The future

- what your short- and long-term objectives are
- what finance you will need for your business and what you will use this for
- what the lender will get out of this deal.

This section will cover one or two pages.

Plan of action

1. Begin gathering together the materials you will need to create a business plan. When you have done this begin putting the information together and keep rewriting the plan until the words flow and are persuasive.

2. Start making contact with organisations that may be able to offer you advice on funding your business or may even provide funds.

3. Start checking out the banks and begin making appointments. Do the same for accountants.

6

Marketing Your Business

'Invent a better mousetrap and the world will beat a path to your door.' Only under the most exceptional circumstances is that true.

When you're in business, you just can't wait for the world to come to you. If you take that attitude, your career as an entrepreneur will be a short one. Instead, you have to promote yourself and very heavily, especially at first, when no one knows you or what you are offering. Therefore it's vital you get your marketing and promotion right, because without sales your business is dead and sooner rather than later. Sales of your product or service are the only thing that contributes to your business; everything else that you do is merely a cost.

One of the worst problems for any entrepreneur, no matter how old or young is the 'Where's my work for Monday morning syndrome?' This question arises especially when you are working on your own. Paradoxically, it is most likely to occur when everything is going well for you.

The problem arises because when you have a lot of work on, you can't be looking for orders at the same time. Therefore, when your current work comes to an end you suddenly find that you have nothing else to do. If you come to a standstill, this might mean a wait of up to two to three months for new income: one month to find it, another month to do it, and yet another month before you get paid.

There is only one answer to this: make sure that you build marketing time into your business day, even when you are at your busiest. And there is no point saying that you don't have time to: you *must*. The more marketing seeds that you sow, the more work you are likely to generate.

There are any number of ways to promote your business, including advertising (radio, television, cinema, the press, directories), direct mail, public relations, exhibitions, telesales and face-to-face selling. Some of these will suit you, your business and your budget, while others won't.

As a new entrepreneur, and with probably limited resources, it will be sensible to select one or two to start with.

How to advertise effectively

When you set up in business, you will probably be buying advertising for the first time. You can avoid many elementary mistakes simply by planning an advertising campaign for yourself, which can be broken into steps.

1. Decide how much you are going to spend on advertising. You should do this in conjunction with the rest of your marketing activity. Remember, advertising isn't the only way to promote your business. You will probably need to spend more on advertising in the early days of your business when no one knows you.

2. Decide when you are going to advertise and where. You will probably think immediately of the local newspaper, but first ask yourself, is it reaching the people who you want to be your customers? If it isn't don't advertise in it. Make a chart of where and when you will advertise as a reminder to yourself.

3. If the local newspaper rings you up and asks you to advertise in their pages (or any one else offering advertising), don't agree automatically. Think the idea through. Will it work for you? Is the advertising at the right price? Can you afford it right now? If you aren't sure, ask the sales rep to call back in an hour or two when you have had time to think about it. And don't be afraid to say no if advertising here isn't right for you.

4. Always keep a check on how effective your advertising is. You can do this either by including a key in your advertise-

ment (for instance you could ask people responding to your ad to write or phone a fictitious person; you would have different names for ads in different publications so that when you hear the name you will know in which paper they have seen the ad; you could code in a spurious department, such as 'Department DT', for ads placed in the *Daily Telegraph*); or you could simply ask anyone you do business with how they heard about you. And if you find that advertising in a particular publication isn't working, drop it from your promotional campaign.

Advertising can be expensive and not very effective, so you must take care that you choose the right publication for your market and weigh up the cost of advertising in it. Depending on your business, it can be difficult to find a publication that is right for you and you will also end up paying to reach people who are not at all interested in what you have to offer.

How to advertise in directories

Many new entrepreneurs think that advertising in directories such as the *Yellow Pages* is very important; and so it can be, but you need to take care in preparing your ads. You will also find that directory advertising is expensive. If you have a business telephone line, you will automatically receive a single line listing in the *Yellow Pages* directory. If you decide to advertise in it (and 96 per cent of 'business information users' are said to look through its pages), the guidelines below should help you. They also apply to advertising in any sort of directory.

● Don't just have a single line entry that gives only your name, address and telephone number as these are very poor when it comes to pulling in business. Think of your own reactions when faced with a long listing like this. Where do you start? So to give readers help in finding you, take the largest display ad that you can afford. This does cost more, but it is far more effective. The extra space will always give you the opportunity to say something about your business and what it can do for the potential customer.

- Also, don't be persuaded ever to run an ad in a newspaper or elsewhere along the lines of 'You'll find us in *Yellow Pages*'. Of course they will, but they'll find all your competitors too. So don't promote the fact that you are in a directory. Directories are for people who haven't seen other forms of advertising.

- Create an ad that works hard for you by using bold graphics and using a strong black box. The telephone number should be as big as possible as this is what directory readers are looking for. Get a designer to design the ad if you can.

- Be careful when writing the words for the ad. Make them mean something. They should emphasise the benefits of using your business.

- Try to use powerful selling words such as You, Money, Save, Results, Guarantee.

- If there is room, try to include an illustration. Photographs are OK if you have the space, but if they are reduced too much they can appear as no more than a black blotch with no detail coming through.

- If your budget runs to it, you could run two smaller ads in different parts of the directory, rather than just the single ad under one heading.

How to organise a mailshot

Sending letters to prospective customers and clients is one of the most cost-effective methods of promoting your business because you are making contact directly with the people you think are most likely to do business with you.

There are two elements to any direct mail campaign. The first is the letter or mailing package you will send out. This needs to be carefully thought out and packed with sales arguments and reasons to buy; in effect the direct mail letter is like a salesperson in an envelope. This can range from just a simple sales letter to more sophisticated and expensive packages.

The second, and equally important, element of the campaign is the list of names and addresses to which you send your letter.

Theoretically, if you send a good sales letter to people who are in the market for your services you will get a good response rate. The main disadvantage you have in promoting your business this way is that the person you want to see your letter may never do so (secretaries often screen the mail for items that they think their bosses won't want to see, for instance). Also, many people are fed up with receiving junk mail and so will immediately consign your mailing to the bin without looking at it. One way around this is to make your mailshot look as much like a personal or standard letter as possible.

You can run your direct mail campaign in two ways. You can either send your letter to lots of names and addresses on a list or else select individuals and businesses and write them a personalised letter. The first approach is more appropriate if you are selling a relatively modestly priced product or service since you will need to promote to a lot more people. To save you time you can buy these names and addresses from mailing list brokers who advertise in the *Yellow Pages* (under 'Direct mail'), or you can make the list up yourself by using local directories and other information sources. Always do a test mailing on part of the list first, and adjust the letter if a reasonable response is not forthcoming until you get it right, before sending out the entire mailshot.

Alternatively, identify those individuals and businesses that you think could do business with you. One way of doing this is to read the local newspapers and other publications and listen to the local radio and television. If you see or hear of anyone you think might need your products and services, write to them explaining why in particular you can help them. The more personal and individual you make the letter the more chance you will have of their becoming a customer. To make this type of mailshot more effective, indicate at the bottom of the letter that you will phone them in a few days to see if you can answer any of their questions. Direct mail campaigns undertaken in this way are very cost effective, but they are time consuming and require a good deal of research.

If you are short of funds, you might consider sharing your

mailing costs with other businesses. Contact them and say that you are organising a mailshot of such and such a number. You would like to incorporate their promotional literature if they will share the mailing costs. You should, of course, choose a company that is not in direct competition with you.

Using public relations to promote your business

Probably the most cost-effective means of promoting your business is to use some well-targeted public relations. Your main purpose will be to get mentions in the press and on the television and radio, by sending them stories about you and your business. Whether the story appears in the press will be dependent on whether the journalist or editor handling it thinks that it is worthwhile and newsworthy enough to print or screen. Unlike advertising in which you are guaranteed your ad appearing in a certain publication on a certain day because you have paid for it, there is no certainty with public relations.

How to make contact with the press

The easiest way to get in touch with the media is to send out a press release. This is the standard way of telling the basics of your story. The best time to send out a press release is when you are launching a new business or a product or service, or have something happening in your company that you think others ought to know about.

There is a recognised way to set out a press release, and an example is shown overleaf.

Your press release will attract more attention if it comes in a stiffened envelope and a photograph is enclosed, together with a typed caption. Black and white photos are best for newspapers, and the quality needs to be sharp and clear for reproduction. The caption can be pasted on the back (never clipped or stapled) and should identify any people in the picture. Even better, send a selection of photos so the editor has a choice.

<u>PRESS RELEASE</u>

<u>LOOK OUT FOR HOUSE WATCH</u>

A new business has been set up by 21-year-old college leaver, Mark Taylor, from Herefordshire, looking after people's properties while they away on holiday or business, whether that is for weeks, months or even just an overnight stay.

House Watch will organise someone to occupy the property while its owners are away and to care for any pets, water plants and make sure that no tell-tale milk bottles or letters are left around for would-be burglars to spot.

'House Watch offers owners the security of knowing that their home is not left unoccupied while they are away', says Mark. 'And it is particularly valuable to people in a rural area, such as this, where you may not have neighbours to keep a look out.'

Though House Watch will initially operate only in Herefordshire, Mark has plans to expand the business region-ally if things go well.

For further information contact Mark Taylor on 01432 123456.

31 August 1995

End

As you can see there are a number of elements to the release.

- The release is headed with the words <u>PRESS RELEASE.</u> This immediately tells a journalist that this is not a standard letter, but could contain valuable news.
- There is a headline at the top of the release. This should indicate the contents of the release. If you can make it witty and eye-catching that's great, but it you can't, don't worry. Just write a straightforward headline, such as NEW BUSINESS BOOK FOR THE UNDER-25s.
- The press release is double spaced. Leaving an extra line between the lines means that there is room for the editor or journalist to edit your release and make notes.
- The first paragraph gives all the important points of the story immediately. Press releases are written like this, because most copy (written material) is cut from the bottom up. Putting all the important information at the top means that nothing that needs to go in the story is likely to be left out. The first paragraph should therefore contain information on *what* the story is about, *who* the story is about, *where* the story took or is taking place, *when* the story took place, *why* the story is taking place or why it is important, and if necessary *how* the story took place. Every press release should answer these what, who, where, when, why (and possibly how) questions. All the subsequent paragraphs of a release just fill out the first paragraph.
- There should be a contact name so that if journalists want more information they have someone to contact.
- And at the end of the release a date should be given and 'End' written so that journalists know they are on the last page of the release and don't need to look for other material. Ideally, the release should fit on to one page of A4 paper, but occasionally you will need to use a second sheet; but no more. If you do use a second sheet then write 'm/f' (more follows) on the bottom of the first sheet and number each page.

Do you have a story?

Whenever you are thinking of sending out a press release you should determine whether you have a story that anyone wants to hear or read about at all. If you can answer most of these questions then go ahead and send a release.

- Is the story topical? That is, does it relate to something that is happening in the news at the moment or has caught the public's imagination?

- Is the story relevant to the readers of the publication? There is no point in writing a press release that tells the world you are marketing snow shoes for huskies and then sending it to a baby magazine! Don't laugh, such things have been known.

- Is there anything different about your story? Again, there is no point sending out a press release if you are a fish-monger who has merely knocked 5p a pound off cod. There has to be something different about the story that makes it worth reading. This difference need not be exceptional; an old story with a new freshness to it will do the job equally well.

Finding help to write your press release

If you find it difficult to write a reasonable press release, there are several cost-effective routes you can take. First, you can contact a local journalist and ask him or her to do it for you. This will have to be a freelance journalist who does not work on the local paper; otherwise you are going to get a conflict of interest.

Where to send it

If yours is a local story, you will already have a pretty good idea of the local publications to which to send your release. But the story may be of a wider interest to the specialist press; so how do you find out where to send it? Thankfully, there are a number of directories which are full of just that sort of information and your local library or business library should hold them. So look out for *Willings Press Guide*, *BRAD*, *Benn's Media*

Directory, *PIMS UK Media Directory*, *The Artists' and Writers' Yearbook* and *The Writer's Handbook*. Each of these gives information on different newspapers and magazines. By working through them you should soon end up with a list of publications that may find your story interesting.

When you have done that send your release to the editor unless the publication is large enough to have different editors or specialist journalists who handle your area or activity.

When sending out press releases, always keep in mind the lead times of the publication you are sending them to. The lead time of a publication is the time before its sale date by which the magazine or newspaper has to be written. For example, you may have to send out press releases in September or October if you want your story to appear in the December issue. If you leave it any later, your news may not be published. Call the publication to find out when they must have copy by.

With all releases safely posted all that remains is for you to sit back and see what happens. Don't be tempted to follow up a press release with a phone call. It won't help. If your story is worth using it will be used, irrespective of a phone call. Likewise, if the story does not appear, don't call the paper and demand to know what happened to the story; that is a sure fire way to alienate the journalist whom you might need as a friend later on in your business career. Also don't ask the publication to send you a cutting of the story if you are fortunate or skilful enough to have your release appear in the press; they won't because they have better things to do, and it will make you look unprofessional.

Good entrepreneurs are highly successful at using the media. You only have to look at Richard Branson to see how well he 'manipulates' the press, not even waiting for a news story to break but actively creating stories which he can tell the press. Therefore you should begin cultivating your press contacts before you need them.

Selling on the phone

Whenever you pick up the phone, you are selling yourself and your business, even if it is an incoming call. How you behave and what you say when on the phone all goes to create an image of your business. During office hours you should take all calls in person if you can, and do so in a friendly but business-like manner. And though it is normal for many people to answer the phone with the telephone number, you should not do this when in business. So, rather than answering with 'Hello, this is Upper Longbottom 123', you should answer with the name of your company and your name, for example, 'Goldleaf Marketing, Henrietta Dobson speaking'. This makes it sound as though your business is larger than it is.

If you work from home and live with others, you should make certain that no one answers with funny quips about this being 'Battersea Dogs Home' and the like. This can be a particular problem when there are young children around. Indeed, young children should never answer the phone during office hours if you can help it.

If people ask you when is a good time to get hold of you on this number, don't just say any time. This does have the advantage of emphasising your availability; however, it also suggests that your time is very flexible and that you don't have a formal structure to your day. Instead, say something like, 'Oh, you can reach me on this number generally between 2 and 3.30'. You are, of course, there the whole time, but people don't realise it. You can use this technique to ensure that you keep calls to a minimum during a particular period of the day when you try to get a lot of uninterrupted work done. By training others to call only after or before a certain time you will be able to get on with your work.

Whenever you talk on the phone you should always smile. This friendliness comes across in your voice; at the same time it also makes you come across as being more natural.

If you have to make a difficult call or sales call, then stand up to do it. This makes you feel more powerful and effective. On the other hand, if you want to come across as being friendly, sit and relax in an easy chair. Both approaches will come across in your voice. And before making a call, always know what you want to say. Jot the main points down on paper first and run the conversation through your head.

Starting your telesales campaign

There are two types of telephone sales call: the cold call and the warm call. Cold calls are made to people you have never contacted before and who know nothing about your business; while warm calls are made to people who have been recommended by someone, or with whom you have had some previous contact. Cold calls are harder to make, but when you are in business they are generally essential. So let's look at some of the techniques that will help you to get the best out of this form of telephone selling.

- Make a list of the people who you think will be most likely to respond positively to your call (for more on prospecting for customers, see below, pages 111–13). But to do this you will need to find out who to call and you can do this in one of two ways.

- Having prospected for the customer you can phone up the switchboard of the company and ask who you need to speak to. The receptionist will attempt to be helpful, but she will probably put you through automatically to a junior in the department, the person who handles all such calls. You won't make much headway here.

- But there is a more effective alternative strategy and that is to phone up the company and ask to speak to the managing director's secretary. Explain the kind of person who you need to speak to and ask her to suggest the name of the person responsible. Because she is at the top of the corporate tree she will know who you should talk to.

- When you phone the person whose name you have been given, say something along the lines of 'I was speaking to your managing director's secretary, Miss Gregson, a few days ago about [outline what the conversation was about] and she suggested that I should talk to you about it'. This creates the impression that you have approval from on high because you appear to have the effective weight of the managing director behind your request.

- So before you make that call, decide what you are going to say and write out a draft script, or at least the main points, on a sheet of paper and have this before you when you make the call. Also, early on in your telephone sales pitch try to ask some questions to which the prospect has to say yes. This helps to encourage a positive attitude towards you. Leave spaces in your sales script to allow for their responses. Remember, you aren't trying to make a sale over the phone but to get an appointment. And try not to give too much information away; face-to-face selling is more effective so you just want to whet the prospect's interest for the moment. You should pay particular attention to the first 20–30 seconds of the call as this is when you will really have to capture the listener's attention.

- Think of any objections that the caller may have and try to think up counter-arguments. Using effective counter-arguments is essentially what persuasive selling is all about. But don't attempt to 'sell' too hard or be overly pushy. This will always count against you and could well result in the phone being put down on you. Try to sell your business by using strong and powerful words that help to bring your sales pitch alive.

- Try to incorporate alternatives into your sales script. So rather than saying, 'Which day of the week would be best for you?', say, 'Would Monday or Tuesday be best for you?'

- When you have done all this, practise what you are going to say and how you will respond to any objections that might arise. The more you prepare before your phone session, the more confident you will be when you start calling.

- Decide on a time when you are going to start phoning and commit yourself to starting then.

- Remember to smile when you phone, stand up to make the call and be enthusiastic.

- Get to the point quickly and don't ramble. Prospects will quickly lose interest if you go all around the houses. For the same reason, keep in mind that this is a sales call and not just a chat.

- If a prospect is negative towards you, don't just say, 'Sorry to have troubled you', and put down the phone. Find out why they aren't interested; it will help you when talking to others and it may lead you to change your sales script.

- If you continue to have trouble on the phone, try creating the impression that you are taking the call on someone else's behalf. The call would therefore begin something like this:

    'Good morning, Mr Kay, my name's Sally Jonson, I'm calling on behalf of Mr Kennedy from Wildebeest Associates. Do you have a moment so I can explain why I've been asked to call?'

    If the prospect says yes then continue by saying something like:

    'Thank you, Mr Kay. Now Mr Kennedy has developed a way for you to [describe briefly how your business, your product or service will help Mr Kay] . . .'

    The benefit of this technique is that *you* aren't doing it, you're just the poor sucker who has been asked by your boss to do something you don't like doing or don't want to do. It also means that if the prospect starts asking awkward questions you can say that 'Mr Kennedy hasn't mentioned that to me, he's not here right now so I can't ask him'.

- If you are phoning from home, ensure that potential distractions are kept to the minimum by shutting pets, children and people out of the room you are calling from.
- If someone asks you to call back in six months why not be a bit cheeky and say, 'Well I have my diary to hand, let's make the appointment now for six months' time'.
- If someone says that they are too busy to see you, offer to meet them at breakfast time, lunch or dinner time.
- During the call take notes about what the prospect is saying.
- When you have sold the prospect on the idea of a meeting, make the appointment for ten minutes or fifteen minutes

to the hour. This suggests that you won't take long. If you do take this approach, make sure that you are on time.

Telephone selling can be very daunting at first, but you need to be brave because it is a very cost-effective means of getting business. And the more you do of it, the more comfortable you will be doing it. Understandably, you probably won't be brilliant on the phone at first, but you will get better. Make small improvements in the way you telephone each week and very soon you will be heading forward at a great pace. If it will help, think of yourself as being like an actor performing to an audience. Read Neil Johnson's book, *Secrets of Telephone Selling*.

Ideally, you should create a weekly call plan so that you are systematic in your selling. Put in one extra call per session. And so that you minimise your travelling time (never forget your time is money), try to group your appointments together in the same area.

Selling in person

Selling face-to-face is one of the areas that many business people feel uncomfortable with, especially younger people who can be intimidated by aggressive and cynical older buyers. However, if you are going to be successful, it is something that you will have to do, otherwise your business will fail.

There are many ideas and thoughts on how to sell to someone face-to-face, so this book can only give so much direction. But as a young entrepreneur bear in mind these few main points.

● Look your very best when you arrive for your meeting by dressing in a professional and business-like manner (see pages 117–18). If you look the part, you will feel more confident about yourself and what you have to offer to the customer or client.

● Arrive for your meeting in plenty of time. Visit the loo to make sure that you are still looking in good shape and to make sure that you don't start feeling uncomfortable during the interview, something that can happen all too easily, especially if you are a bit nervous. You can also help to calm your nerves by learning a few relaxation techniques and remembering to breathe slowly and deeply.

- If you are running late for an appointment, call the client's secretary and explain that you are running ten minutes late, ask them to convey your apologies to the client and say that you will be there soon.
- When you enter the meeting room be friendly and confident. The first few minutes of any meeting are crucial. If the client doesn't like you now, he or she is unlikely to do business with you.
- Plan what you are going to say and do before meeting the prospective client or customer and especially answers to any awkward questions that the client might ask you. This will give you extra confidence. Sell the idea of what you have to offer by concentrating on the benefits to the client of using it. To do this you need to know the difference between a feature and a benefit. For example, you would not sell a drill bit by saying that it was $^3/_8$ inch diameter (a feature), but that it made $^3/_8$ inch holes, which is what the customer wants. The fact that the bit makes this size hole is the benefit.
- Always be flexible in your approach and be prepared to negotiate; remember you are the boss.
- If the client says they don't want what you have to offer, find out why that is, if possible.
- At the end of the interview, particularly if the client has agreed to do business with you, ask him or her if they know someone else (a supplier, or a colleague in the same company perhaps) who might also be interested in what you have to offer. This is known as asking for a referral. When you have this other person's name you can phone them up and quite legitimately say that Mr Smith or Mrs Jones suggested that you contact them.

Marketing with leaflets

This is a very cost-effective means of promotion, but you

should expect a low response rate from your efforts, as leafleting is really a numbers game. The more you put out, the more response you will get. You can leaflet to all manner of people: shoppers, business people, car owners, shopkeepers, train travellers, tourists, theatre-goers. You can either slot leaflets through letterboxes, hand them out to people or leave them at a central point where they can be picked up. You will see many leaflets stuck under car windscreen wipers; though little is ever said about this, you should be aware that strictly speaking it is illegal.

Do you need a brochure?

Not every business will need a brochure (leafleting might provide a more cost-effective weapon) though most service businesses will find it a very effective promotional tool provided it is well thought out, well written and well designed. The big mistake many start-up businesses make (and for that matter well-established ones) is to try and make the brochure appeal and to sell to far too many people. This may seem cost-effective but this blunderbuss approach means that people can get confused about what you are offering, or think that you are offering so much that you can't be good at it all. So think what you want your brochure to do.

Your brochure is a selling document for your business that should attract potential clients to find out more. It will be the rare customer who is so impressed by your brochure that they will buy from you in any case. So the main aim of the brochure must be to tell people what your business is all about and why it will benefit them. You will need to decide who you want to tell all this to, so think of your ideal type of customer and then a couple of other customers whose needs aren't quite the same, but similar. These will be the potential customers that your brochure should be talking to.

Now you need to give your brochure a 'personality' that reflects and promotes your business. This personality will be created by what you write in the brochure, the style of that writing and the design of the brochure. Bear all this in mind and refer back to your initial thoughts on what image you and your business want to have.

Finding more customers

You need to be continually looking for new prospects either because you are losing customers or because you want more in order to expand the business; and remember marketing your business is largely a numbers game. If you need to telephone six people to get one appointment and you need to see six people to make one sale, you will have to telephone 36 people to get one sale. The longer it takes you to make contact with 36 people, the longer it will take to make that one sale.

Local newspapers are one of the best sources of information on prospective clients and customers so you should read all the locals every week. Be on the lookout not just for relevant general news stories but also those that apply to companies. Particularly informative pages in the paper are the classified ads as these tell you which local companies are looking for new employees (because they are expanding and may need your products or services) or are changing personnel (new staff might want to implement new plans, or bring in new equipment providing a sales opportunity for you).

Yellow Pages and the *Thomson Directory* are good sources for developing a basic list of companies who may be interested in doing business with you. However, you will need to do a little extra work if you are mailing to them as generally the full address and postcode are not given. You will therefore need to look these up in the postcode directories you will find alongside the *Yellow Pages* in most reference libraries.

National directories will also give you information about local companies as these are generally categorised by locality. The librarian at your local reference library, particularly if it has a business section, will be able to point you in the direction of the most valuable of these, such as Kompass.

When you are searching for new customers, look first for the people that you *want* to have as clients and customers. Though you might think early on that you'll do business with anyone (to an extent this is true), why attempt to do business with people with whom you don't feel comfortable, who you think might be troublesome, or for whom you think you might not be able to do the best of jobs. You will generally find that this still leaves you with a lot of prospective clients and customers.

Use your existing customers to find others by always asking for referrals (their suppliers, business friends, or other people within their company) who might find your services or products beneficial.

Keep up with old contacts, and stay in touch with ex-colleagues and friends: you may be of mutual benefit; they will also help to stop you from becoming isolated. Don't wait until you want something before contacting people: this looks as though you are using them; send them information and chat with them before you need them.

If you are working but want to go self-employed try to ensure that your current employer, or previous ones, become your first client.

Use any personal contacts you may have. Tell as many people as possible that you know about what you are going to do. Get them to pass the word around and to keep their eyes and ears open for possible opportunities for you to do business. Ask your family and friends for their ideas about whom to make contact with.

And don't just throw away the mailshots that come through your door, but look carefully at them. Is there a client or customer among them who may need your services? They obviously want more business, so if the mailshot is successful they may be in the market.

You should always be positive in your approach to all your marketing activity. Customers may not be thick on the ground, but you must believe that there is a new customer or client just around the corner. So be aggressive in your marketing and double your efforts.

How to improve your marketing success rate

1.   Identify more prospects.

2.   Get in the habit of asking for more and more referrals.
3.   Try to increase the quality of these prospects.
4.   Choose the best prospects who are most likely to do business with you first.
5.   Call, write and speak to more of these prospects.
6.   See more of these prospects.
7.   Improve your sales techniques.
8.   Don't concentrate just on existing customers. Always be looking to enter and exploit new markets.
9.   Always ask yourself how can you adapt your products or services to different markets and customers.

Plan of action

1.   Develop your social life. Begin networking with people who may be able to help you. This is a very cost-effective means of marketing yourself and your business because all it involves is talking and meeting with people, letting them know you are around and at the same time creating a mutual support group. You can network by attending meetings of a local business club and going on training courses.

2.   Try to do some sales or marketing activity every day, or if you can't or don't want to, then do some at least twice a week. This could be anything, ranging from writing a simple sales letter to making a phone call, or gaining some new referrals.

3.   Start making a list of those people and companies you can contact now in your search for business. Visit the local library and begin working through the local and national directories.

4.   Start reading as many books as you can about selling and marketing. Make sure that these are practical books with lots of ideas and different approaches. Some suggested titles are listed in Chapter 10.

5.   If you are currently working for someone else, but want to

go self-employed, begin looking for clients months before you leave your job.

6.   Begin collecting other businesses' letterheads. Analyse them and work out what elements about them are good and what bad. Are there elements that you could use in your own letterheads? Do the same for business cards.

7.   Begin thinking of logo designs.

8.   Start looking at other businesses and decide what images they have.

9.   Buy a small notebook, call this your Contacts Book and begin filling it with local journalists whose names you see in the papers and other people who you think might be of use to you. Make a note of what it is they do or have done, and how you think they may be of help to you.

7

Creating Your Business Image

The saying 'You can't judge a book by its cover' may be true, but unfortunately many people still do it all the same, even in the business world. Lord King of British Airways didn't take Richard Branson seriously 'because he wore a sweater' and look who came out on top.

That just goes to prove that customers, clients, suppliers and other business people will expect certain things from you and one of these expectations will be that you appear business-like. That means they will expect you to dress, look and behave in a certain way. If you don't have that 'look of business' right now, then how are you seen?

This chapter is all about creating the right image, but to do that you really need to know how others see you. When you know that, it's usually far easier to plot a route to where you want to be. So let's begin this chapter with a little bit of personal stock-taking.

How do others see you?

First, take a large sheet of paper and write down all the things that you think about yourself. You should already have thought deeply about this when assessing yourself in Chapters 1 and 2. The sort of thing you might write about yourself is friendly, ambitious, relaxed, always smiling, firm handshake, sociable, healthy-looking, optimistic and so on; as many as you can think of.

Now write them down in a list on A4 paper and leave a space next to each one. If you do the list in two columns, you could probably get it on to one sheet of A4. If you can, type it. Then make some photocopies.

Next, ask as many of your friends and acquaintances to help you as you feel able to. You could, if you wish, dress it up as a sociology experiment. Ask a whole range of people from your best and oldest friends and your family to relatively minor acquaintances. Give each a copy of your questionnaire. Ask each to tick those characteristics that they agree with and add their own characteristics if they can think of any more or any of a better description. To avoid embarrassment to them, they can make their replies anonymously. But you should nevertheless code each questionnaire you give out with a code from 1 to 5, with 1 being those who know you best and 5 being those who know you least.

When the questionnaires have been returned, analyse the results. You may be in for a surprise. Look particularly at the following matters:

- In general, how many agreed with your own assessment of yourself? Do they see you as you see yourself?
- What additional characteristics did they come up with? Do any additional descriptions occur regularly? If so, your respondents may have a point.
- Look at those particular characteristics that a business person requires. Do people think that you have these characteristics? If not, you need to work on those areas.
- Sort the responses out into a range from those who know you best to those who know you least. Do any patterns emerge from this? For example, if you only appear confident and optimistic to those who have known you a long time, this will not help you with scarcely met business acquaintances.

This exercise will highlight those areas of your image that you particularly need to work on to impress your business acquaintances.

Choosing your image

The image you want should be an extension of what you are now. You shouldn't try to change your image too much too soon; to do so would look false, you would not be able to keep it up, and you would be uncomfortable in what you were doing. If you think you need to make a radical change in your image, think about doing this in stages by changing just one aspect of your appearance or general image at a time.

You can have different images for different people or groups of people. For example, if your customers are generally young you may want to dress in a more relaxed way so that they feel 'you are one of them'. But dressing that way wouldn't be sensible if you were having a meeting with the bank manager, when a more formal approach would be best. However, dress differently from others if you want to set yourself apart from them and to appear more dynamic.

Choosing the right clothes

When you are in business, the important thing is to wear the clothes that are right for the job and for the occasion. Overalls are for the workshop and not to see the bank manager. If you run a service business, particularly one in which you need to inspire confidence in others that you can do the right job, it's especially important to create the right image. To do that you don't necessarily need a suit, but a smart pair of trousers and jacket for men or a skirt and jacket for women are a minimum.

When choosing your business clothes you should not be too fashion-conscious, but should aim rather for styles that are classics. If you aren't quite sure what these styles are, take a walk along the streets at rush hour and see what business people are wearing as they go to work. Also start looking through fashion and lifestyle magazines. There are also a number of books published on better dressing; a suggested start is *The Image Factor* by Eleri Sampson (Kogan Page).

Now with some ideas in your head, wander around clothes shops and begin creating new wardrobes in your head. When you finally come to buy, choose a few good quality clothes that will keep their shape and look good rather than going for a lot of cheaper clothes that lose their shape and quickly look tatty. The better the look of your clothes, the more confident you will feel.

And after you have bought them, make sure that your clothes are always clean, pressed and well looked after. Hang your clothes up after wearing them so they stay uncreased. This is also good discipline, so do it no matter how tired you are at the end of a day.

If you want to add some character to your business clothes, you can always do so by choosing shirts that have different coloured collars, interesting ties and cuff links, or attractive brooches or ear rings. Make sure that you have two pairs of shoes so you have a standby pair when one pair needs mending.

Improving your 'business' voice

You don't need to talk posh to be in business; indeed that can be a disadvantage; but the more powerful and interesting your voice, the more confident and persuasive you will be, especially when making sales presentations and trying to win some business. Most people's voices could do with a little work on them, so begin putting the following into practice:

- If you are serious about improving the quality of your voice, choose a person to learn from. This could be someone you know, but it is easier to choose someone you hear regularly on television or radio. Repeat phrases and sentences that they say trying to copy the style of their speech. Don't attempt to mimic them and be careful to choose someone whose voice you feel comfortable with. You don't want to end up with a voice that sounds obviously false or forced.
- Practise speaking carefully, precisely and clearly from a book in front of the mirror. Most people are self-conscious about this, so wait until no one's around before doing this as it's important that you open your mouth properly and don't mumble when doing this. Try to get an up-and-down rhythm to your voice as this makes it more interesting. Think of how the good speaker you are copying talks.

- If you have one, take a tape recorder and record yourself reading a page or two from this book. When you have finished play the tape back. Yes, that really is how you speak. Now what are the good points and bad points about your voice? What do you think? What do others think? Is it lazy, does it sound slurred, nervous, hesitant, too loud or too soft? Now read the same pages again but bear these points in mind: make a real effort to open your mouth a little wider than you do normally. Your throat will feel a little more open too; smile; and then try to alter the tone of your voice so that it goes up and down. Listen to the tape again. Now doesn't that sound better? Keep practising.

- Read some books on voice control and pay particular attention to what they have to say about breathing. If you are more serious about developing your voice, consider taking lessons from a voice coach.

- When you feel more confident about your voice, take every opportunity to speak in front of others, just small groups at first, but then larger groups as you feel more comfortable.

- If your voice tends to rise and your words become more rapid when you speak, make a conscious effort to slow down your breathing and to take deeper breaths. Relax your shoulders as you do so. Also make a deliberate effort to slow down your speech. If you are still rushing your words, practise taking a few deep breaths (not too obviously) between sentences.

Building up your confidence

Appearing confident, even if you are not, is very important in being a successful entrepreneur, so the more confidence you have the better. There are a number of ways in which you can develop your confidence.

You must start thinking that you *can* become more confident. Remember that everyone feels nervous from time to time, even politicians when under the television spotlight or centre stage. The difference is that they have learned to control their nerves so well that you will never know.

Your first step should be to identify someone who exudes a lot of confidence. This should be someone you see regularly in real life or on television. Choosing someone on the box is better because you look at them closely and also record them, playing back the images again and again. Study how they move, the signals that they give off that say 'I am confident and in control'. Start copying these mannerisms, gestures and postures. Do this until you are doing it comfortably and without thinking.

Next, make an extra special effort to get as good as you possibly can be at your chosen business. Then you know that if anyone doubts that you are competent to do a job, you *know* you are. Being certain that you can do the job is a great confidence builder.

Even if you are short, always try to walk talk, with your shoulders back and chest out. People who walk around with their shoulders slouched give the impression that they are uncertain, lack confidence and have a weak personality.

Minding your (body) language

You may believe that you are a millionaire-in-waiting but if your body is telling everyone you meet the complete opposite, that you are uncomfortable and lack confidence, are they going to believe you? Most unlikely. Not only the way that we talk but the way that we move gives off an image of success, or lack of it. So, particularly as a young entrepreneur, you must work on ensuring that what you are saying is not undermined by what your body is subconsciously saying.

Avoid the following mannerisms if you want to come across as a sincere, confident and well thought of business person:

- Fidgeting and displaying excessive mannerisms such as twiddling your thumbs when sitting in a chair at interviews and meetings. Instead, sit back in the chair but make sure that you aren't slouching by sitting forward rather than back. Clasp your hands together in front of you, letting them lie on your lap. If you want to do something with your hands, you can always take notes of what they are saying, but only do this if it is appropriate and try not to doodle on the page.

● Putting your hands up to your face. Tapping your nose, rubbing at your ear lobes or eyes are all thought to be indications that you are telling lies.

● Taking off your glasses and cleaning them in the middle of the meeting, or lighting up a pipe or a cigarette, even if this is acceptable. These come across as being stalling tactics, designed to gain you time.

● Folding your arms in front of you. This makes you look defensive, as if you have something to hide.

● Using both your hands to hold a bag or cup in front of you. This looks weak and suggests that you might be feeling unsure of yourself. Put cups and bags down on tables or the floor if you have the chance.

Always remember that these gestures work two ways, so look out for them in the people you are doing business with. So keep a watch on their facial expressions, hand movements and body position and take confidence from the fact that they may be more nervous than you are.

However, when in meetings, don't be frightened to use your hands and arms to make gestures as these help to emphasise your sales points. Don't go overboard, though. Looking like a human windmill as you go through your sales pitch is more off-putting than business-winning.

Also, when you are talking to a client, or would-be customer, you will often find that your eyes drift away into the middle distance, which is perfectly normal. Now before answering a question or making a point, bring your eyes back to look at and focus on the client, pause, and then say what you have to. This makes you appear more serious and your words more thoughtful.

And as a customer makes points to you, smile and nod at each one. This makes the customer feel that you understand his needs and are in tune with his thinking. Smile as you speak and be as enthusiastic as you can. If you aren't enthusiastic about what you are offering and saying to a customer, how can they be?

When it comes to important items, such as talking about figures, it is time for a more serious approach, in which case lower your voice. It is crucial to appreciate when to make this change between being light-hearted and being serious. Being in business is about making money and if you appear flippant at an inappropriate time, customers and clients will begin to have doubts about how serious you are.

What about your car?

Old bangers are great for just getting around. And because your friends are probably no better off than yourself, the look, make and model of your car doesn't matter at all to them. In business it can and does. So, if you don't have a good car, and don't have the cash to buy another one, what can you do? Quite bluntly the answer is don't make the failings of your car obvious.

- Always, but especially if it is an 'old banger', make sure that your car is regularly serviced so there is less chance of it going wrong. If you don't then Sod's Law will dictate that your car won't start on the very morning that you have to meet an important client to clinch a deal.
- Join the AA or RAC or another reputable breakdown and recovery organisation. This at least gives you a fall-back position should anything go wrong.
- If your car is liable to breaking down make some back-up arrangements to borrow friends' cars before yours causes you a problem.
- If you are off to a meeting then try starting your car an hour or more before you have to go. Of course, there is no guarantee that it will start when you are ready to leave, but at least this way you will have a bit more time if cold or wet overnight weather has affected the battery.
- Leave for your meeting in plenty of time, then if there is a problem, you have some leeway.
- If you do drive to a client's in an old banger, park it around the corner where it won't be seen. There is no

reason to flaunt your car's failings. If you do have to park in the client's car park, put the car out of direct line of sight of the windows. You don't want your client to see you getting in or out of it.

● When in the meeting, never make any comment about your car or bring the subject up at all.

Creating an image for your business

Creating the right image for your business, as well as yourself, is vitally important in attracting the right customers and clients. Very early on you should decide what image you want for yours. Do you want to be seen as modern, old-fashioned, high-tech, low-tech, offering a high level of service, speedy delivery, highly innovative, dependable, reliable, small, large, responsible? In reality you will probably want a combination of a number of such characteristics. And two of the most significant vehicles for getting across your business image are your business name and your business stationery.

Designing your stationery

Every business needs quality stationery because it makes you look professional. A letterhead is just a sheet of A4 with your business name, address, telephone and fax number and perhaps a logo on it. It is worth spending a lot of time getting your letterhead right as this creates a certain image immediately for your business; it is also for many the first thing that they see from you, and first impressions do count. A letter is like a company's sales rep who arrives by post. Bear in mind the following points:

● Your letterhead should be in keeping with the image you have chosen for your business, so its overall appearance needs to suggest that you are business-like, professional, and able to offer quality. No one is impressed by a cheap piece of stationery that suggests you will do a runner as soon as you get the client's or customer's money and to hell with the job. Your letterhead should always make people feel confident about using your services.

- Add a line to your letterhead which states what your business is about; for instance, 'Creative public relations and publicity', 'High quality graphic design', or 'In-depth market research'. These act as sales messages and give the recipient of the letter a little more reason to use you rather than someone else.

- It always pays to have your letterhead professionally designed. Ask other business people to recommend someone who has done a good job. Or if you see a letterhead that you like, phone up the business and find out who designed it. As a less costly alternative, you can approach a tutor at the local design or arts college and offer this as a project that his or her students can work on.

- When you are buying your letterheads also think in terms of the envelopes and continuation sheets (which you use when sending out more than one sheet) which should be in a similar style, with a common design element, such as a logo.

- Finally, when you have had your letterheads delivered, keep control of them. You don't want people sending letters out on your behalf.

Designing your business cards should be done with the same care and attention as designing letterheads. Indeed, the design of both should be done together so that both letterheads and business cards look obviously part of the family. Again, have a slogan on your business card. Don't be tempted to go for unusual sizes, as people will find it difficult to put them in the standard wallets for business cards. Credit-card size is fine, though you may like to have one that stands upright (has its short edges at the top and bottom) rather than horizontal (long edges at top and bottom).

Once you have your business cards, always make sure that you have a good supply on you. Business cards are no good when they are left in the drawer.

You may feel that at this early stage you don't need compliment slips. You are probably right. If you need to include a note with something you mail out then you can always use a letterhead as it is or cut one down in size until it is like a comps slip.

Plan of action

1. Do the image questionnaire exercise detailed at the beginning of this chapter to find out how others see you. If the questionnaire highlights any problems, take the appropriate steps to remedy those problems.

2. Try out the voice exercise detailed on pages 118–19 to see how your voice can be improved; and make those improvements.

3. Start thinking about the design of your business stationery. Do some preliminary sketches of possible designs, and mull them over. Get some quotes from designers and printers.

4. If you need more business-like clothes, decide when you are going to start shopping for new ones. Write down that date now.

5. Read books on developing confidence and put their ideas into practice; they will help you to acquire relaxation skills that will keep you from getting tense and anxious.

6. Join some sports and leisure clubs that interest you and become involved. Make the effort to talk to as many people as possible in these informal environments. Try to speak to at least one new person every day and to tell them that you are in business and what it is. The more you do this, the more confidence you will gain about the whole idea of being in business.

8

How to Work Smarter

How successful you are in business depends on you and no one else. You are the one who has to do things, make decisions, plan your activities and organise the time to do all of this. This self-management is one of the most important elements of entrepreneurship. This chapter looks at a number of techniques to help you get the best out of yourself. So let's begin by finding out when you work best.

Lark or an owl?

If you work for yourself then to some extent you do have the advantage of being able to work when you want. And if you do have this opportunity, it is foolish not to take advantage by working the hours that you want to, even if they do not fit in with the conventional working day.

Now you will probably have discovered that there are times during the day when you work and function better than other times. Some people are 'larks' who work better in the morning while others are 'owls' who are best at night. If you are not sure whether you are an owl or a lark, try the following exercise.

For a week fill in the table shown below, by ringing the number in each line that most accurately describes the way you are feeling at that time. Do this for every two-hour period. So for instance, if you are feeling alert and energetic at 7am circle the 1 for that time, but if you feel slow then circle the 4 for that time.

By the end of a week, for each time there should consistently be a particular level of alertness circles giving you a pattern for

Your Sleep/Alertness Table								
	6–8	8–10	10–12	12–2	2–4	4–6	6–8	8–10
Alert and energetic	1	1	1	1	1	1	1	1
Alert but not at peak	2	2	2	2	2	2	2	2
Awake, not fully alert	3	3	3	3	3	3	3	3
Sluggish	4	4	4	4	4	4	4	4

the week. If you have circled a lot of 1s in the morning then you are a lark, but if 1s are circled in the evening then you are more likely to be an owl. Many people will not come across as being either strongly an owl or a lark.

How do you waste time?

Whether you are a lark or an owl, like everybody else in this world you still have only 24 hours in a day; so the better you can use the time, the more successful you will be in achieving what you want. Consequently good entrepreneurs don't waste time. Run through the following list and identify the most common and important time wasters in your business life.

Do you have to hunt around on your desk looking for things?Yes/No

If someone calls on the phone do you talk longer than is necessary?
Yes/No

If someone calls, do you break off work to chat or do you tell them that you are busy? Yes/No

Do you tend to take breaks in the day that are too frequent and too long? Yes/No

Do you break away from your work to read articles in newspapers or magazines? Yes/No

Do you try to do several jobs at once rather than concentrating on one at a time? Yes/No

Are you continually looking for reasons to leave your workplace or desk? Yes/No

---

How valuable is your time?

It's said that time is money, so try working out how much money you lose if you do waste time by doing something else. The table below gives an indication but you can work it our for your own needs. The calculations are based on a 40-hour week and 48 working weeks to the year.

Income	Hourly rate	Minute rate	The cost of wasting 15 minutes a day over a year
£15,000	£ 7.81	13.0p	£ 468.00
£20,000	£10.41	17.3p	£ 622.80
£25,000	£13.02	21.7p	£ 781.20
£30,000	£15.62	26.0p	£ 936.00
£45,000	£23.44	39.0p	£1406.25

And how many of us will waste *just* 15 minutes each day. The cost of this wasted time is even higher when you work for yourself because not all of that 40-hour week is productive time; much of it won't earn you a penny. For example, if you earn for 25 hours of the week, the rest being taken up in marketing and administrative chores, then if you earn an income of £45,000, the wasted time would amount to £2250!

Using lists

One of the best way to ensure that you do everything that you have to do is to make a list. Having tasks to do written in black and white not only gives you physical evidence of what must be done, but induces a pang of guilt when you don't do it. The following points should help you make better lists.

- Spend 15 minutes at the end of each day writing out a list of things to do for the next day. Call this List 1.
- Once a week write out a list of all the longer-term jobs that you have to do, such as prepare a proposal, write a sales brochure or look for new premises. Then break each

of these large tasks into smaller jobs, which can be done in a few minutes, an hour or a day. Call this List 2.

● Then create your final 'To Do' list by mixing jobs from List 1 and List 2 so that it contains small and large tasks, those that have to be done on that particular day, and also jobs that are part of your longer-term plans.

● If you wish, you can then run down that list, prioritising items, giving each an A (important), B (not so important) or C (bottom of the pile jobs), depending on how important each job is. A quicker method of prioritising the list is simply to choose the most important item on the list and do it. When you have finished, choose the next most important item until you have finished the list.

● Once you have chosen to do an item on the list, the only thing that remains is to do it.

● Don't make your lists too long. If you do, you won't have finished everything on it by the end of the day and you will become demoralised. If you do have any items left on the list, transfer them to the next day. If you find that you are transferring the same items over from day to day, you are probably guilty of procrastination, constantly deferring these jobs.

As you become more adept at making lists and using them, you will develop your own personal preferences and find ways of adapting these rules to suit these preferences.

Your daily schedule

If you are working on your own and for yourself it can be very easy to be distracted. No one is looking over your shoulder to see that you do your work and with that lack of discipline you can end up doing activities that aren't productive, profitable or even anything to do with your business. Therefore you should create a rigid framework for your day by trying to plan 60–70 per cent of your time. Don't try to plan all your day, but leave room for the unexpected to happen, which gives you flexibility.

You will need two things to begin creating your schedule: your To Do list and a sheet of A4 paper (a good conservation measure is to use the back of junk mail). On the paper draw up a grid similar to the one shown here.

Daily timetable		Date
Start	To Do	Duration (minutes)
8.00		
8.10		
8.20		
8.30		
8.40		
8.45		
9.00		
9.15		
9.30		
9.45		
9.50		
10.00		
10.15		

This shows the time periods you are going to divide the day into (these could be 10, 15, 20 or 30 minute blocks) on the left-hand side. Don't choose longer periods than this as you can't concentrate at any one time for much longer and you won't have the flexibility.

If you want, you can use different time blocks for different parts of the day. Perhaps dividing the first hour into 10 minute blocks if this is when you do 'bitty' stuff, before moving on to 30-minute blocks until lunch when you are concentrating on bigger jobs and then using 15-minute blocks in the afternoon when you are becoming more tired and losing your concentration.

Next, look down your To Do list and estimate how long it will take to complete each item. Decide if you want or have to finish that job all in one go or can split it up. When you have done this, begin filling in the grid with the tasks to be done. Try to schedule your workload so that you are doing the most difficult jobs when you are at your most alert either mentally or physically. Why waste all your 'good time' on monotonous and low-grade jobs such as opening the mail or sticking stamps on envelopes?

When you are working in the longer time blocks, every 40 to 45 minutes or so you should include a five or ten minute 'rest block', especially if you are working at the computer. Don't wait until you are tired before taking the break.

You don't actually have to take a rest during these periods, just do something different. A change is as good as a rest. But don't go away and do something that is going to take longer than your break; otherwise you'll be in the middle of it and want to keep on going rather than getting back to what you were doing originally.

When you are sitting at your desk, you should also take 30 or 40 seconds out every ten minutes or so, just to have a quick stretch or move your position. This will make you feel fresher and more alert as well as relaxing you.

Don't believe *Wall Street* – that lunch is for wimps. Try to take a break of 45 to 60 minutes around midday. If you have to skip lunch, don't do so regularly as it will show in your afternoon performance.

If you have to travel to meetings, leave enough time for the travelling. If you have several meetings in the day, make sure that they aren't back-to-back, that is, for example, one finishing at three and the next starting at four. If you do, you will worry about the first meeting overrunning and not give it your full attention. If it does overrun, you will arrive hot and flustered for the second.

When you have created your timetable it will look something like this.

Daily timetable		Date	
Start	To Do	Duration (minutes)	
8.00	Open Mail	10
8.10	Write sales letter	
8.20	Write sales letter	
8.30	Write sales letter	30
8.40	Break	5
8.45	Complete price quote	
9.00	Complete price quote	30
9.15	Phone calls	15
9.30	Prepare for meeting	15
9.45	Break	5
9.50	Work on accounts	
10.00	Work on accounts	
10.15	Work on accounts	25

Set deadlines for yourself

Another great means of ensuring that you get work done is to set yourself deadlines, times by which you must have finished a job or a section of it. For example, you might tell yourself that you have to finish a letter by three o'clock this afternoon, that you will be through with a meeting in ten minutes. However, when you are setting these deadlines, be realistic. If you aren't, you will always miss the deadline and become disillusioned with yourself; and that's no good at all.

You can set different lengths of deadlines, some for your everyday activities and some for your longer-term ones. Deadlines for these you should write down on a sheet of paper and pin it up on the wall to act as a reminder. As an added incentive, why not tell relatives and friends what your longer-term deadlines are and encourage them to ask you how you are getting on with the job?

For a little added incentive, buy a clockwork timer and work against this. Then break each job into convenient blocks of time, say 30 or 40 minutes, and try to finish the job before the bell of the timer goes off.

Managing your phone time

The telephone is a fantastic business tool, but most start-up entrepreneurs won't use it properly, wasting time and effort in the process. So try to organise your phone activity along the following lines:

1. Do your daily phone calls in batches. Once you have picked up the phone, don't put it down until you have finished making all the calls that you are going to do in that batch. This saves you quite a lot of time and stops you being distracted by something else between calls.

2. Write down a list of the phone numbers that you are going to make so that you don't have to hunt for numbers after each call.

3. Plan the calls that you are going to make by writing down what you are going say before you pick up the phone.

4. Jot down the main points of telephone calls as you go along. You can also use a dictaphone or tape recorder to do this. You don't need to tell the other person you are recording the call unless you want to. If you have a hand-held recorder you will need to buy a sucker microphone which you can stick on the handset.

5. Don't hold on for people if they are busy when you call. This wastes time. Offer to call back but don't leave your name and number, otherwise you'll wait in expectation of the call and give them power by allowing them to decide if they are going to phone you back or not.

6. Use the fax as much as possible for short messages, especially if you are just sending information and not needing a reply.

7. Screen calls by using the answer machine, then you can decide if you really want to talk to the caller. People can be put off if they think you are doing this the whole time.

Sometimes it is better not to pick up but to call back, then callers don't know you are screening.

Get more out of your working day

It's easier to achieve your business ambitions if you know what you want. Therefore you should continually set yourself a series of targets; these are your goals. You should have a mixture of short- and long-term goals that can be achieved in a day, week, month or year. For example, you might have goals for marketing which might include making at least *one* telephone sales call every day, writing *ten* sales letters every week, pulling in *three* new customers every month or increasing your sales by £20,000 by the end of the year. Goals mean that at the end of every day you should be able to ask yourself 'What did I want to achieve today/this week/month/year? Did I do it?'

Having goals is good for you and your business, but goals need to be chosen with care if you are to get the most out of them. Therefore, when you are setting goals, consider the following.

- Goals should be *specific*. If they aren't, you won't really know what you are aiming for, or when you have reached it. Therefore, you must make your goals specific by placing actual numbers against them ('raising sales to £60,000' for instance, and not, 'I want to increase sales a lot').

- Your goals must be *measurable*, so that you have a way to gauge your progress. Money is a good yardstick but it could be number of customers, outlets or products made.

- Goals have to be *achievable*. It's no good having ones that are so unrealistic you can't possibly reach them. Saying that you want to have taken over the Virgin Group in six months time may mark you out to be highly ambitious, but it isn't an achievable goal.

- A *time* element also needs to be included. Saying that you will make £6,000 extra sales in the next two months is a different proposition from making an extra £6,000 in the next 12 months.

- When setting daily goals, attempt to include tasks which move you towards achieving your weekly, monthly and yearly ambitions.
- When you have decided upon your goals write them down.
- Try to set increasingly difficult goals that force you to push yourself more and more.

How to make better decisions

Whatever type of business you are in, you will frequently have to make decisions about what to do. In fact, good decision-making is one of the most important skills and abilities for any business person to acquire. And though some decisions are more important than others, they can generally all be made more easily, successfully and confidently by using the following decision-making framework.

1. Identify the decision that you have to make. For example, should I buy a new computer or a second-hand one?
2. Obtain as much information as possible about the situation. The more information you have, the better informed will be your decision. Check that the information is accurate and reliable. Making a decision based on the wrong information does no one any good, no matter how well you go about it. However, if the decision is a difficult one to make, be careful you don't put off making it by using this information-gathering process as an excuse.
3. Ask others (including clients, customers, suppliers, family, friends and other business people) for their suggestions, advice and ideas on what to do. This is another element of the information-gathering process.
4. Next, take a sheet of paper and divide it into two vertical columns. In one column write down all the advantages of making a certain decision that you can think of; then on the other side write down all the disadvantages of making this decision. Usually one side will have far more points than the other and this is usually the right decision to make.

5.   Work out all the possible solutions to the problem that you can think of (ask others so that you don't miss any) and the likely consequences of making that particular decision.

6.   Don't be frightened to make decisions going on your gut reaction, as sometimes these can be the best ones, especially when you are dealing with people that you think may be a bit dubious or dodgy.

7.   Finally, if you do make a bad decision, don't think of this as being a failure, but do your very best to learn from it.

Speed-up/slow-down technique

One technique that may help you to achieve more during the day is 'interval working'. This is similar to interval training in athletics. You use it by setting say a ten-minute period when you will try to work as quickly as possible, doing everything at double speed, almost running to filing cabinets and the like, then slowing back to 'normal speed' for an hour and then 'sprinting' again. This is not something to be tried too frequently but it does add a bit of spice to your working day.

How well are you doing?

From time to time you should check just how productive you are to ensure you are not wasting time or doing unnecessary jobs or other activities. One way of doing this is to keep a time log. Divide a sheet of paper into four columns. At the top of the first write 'STARTED', at the top of the second write 'FINISHED', at the top of the third write 'ACTIVITY', and at the top of the fourth column write 'TOTAL (minutes)'. You should now have something like this:

STARTED	FINISHED	ACTIVITY	TOTAL (minutes)

This is your time log and you should tape it to the top of your desk (to your right-hand side if you are right-handed and the left if you are left-handed). Now, whenever you start doing something write down the time you started and the job on the log. When you stop doing that job write down the time you finished. To make this an effective exercise you should log *everything* that you do during the day, and this includes breaks, interruptions, everything. You may find this a little tedious and time-consuming at first, but you will quickly fall into the routine and it will end up taking no more than a few seconds.

At the end of the day add up how much time you have spent doing each activity. Then add all the work elements together to find out how much time you actually spent working. You will probably be horrified to find that it is nowhere near as much as you think. But this should highlight areas where you are wasting time.

Doing what you put off

There is a Spanish proverb that says, 'Tomorrow is the busiest day of the week', and if you are a great 'putter-offer' then it probably will be. Putting off something that you know you need to do is called procrastination. And there are very real dangers in postponing things which can throw your business off the rails. For example:

- You don't call a person who has some information you need; when you do call, you are desperate and they are out.
- On Thursday you have the time but put off writing a sales letter that you need to send out the next day. But on Friday there is a disaster, you are tied up all day with the supplier. No time to write that letter. You lose the sale.
- A customer needs a quote for work by the end of next week. You have the time to put the quote together this week but because you have ten days to do it in, you don't bother. An opportunity is missed to impress the client by delivering the quote over a week early.

These are just a few of the reasons not to hold back from doing something. If you find yourself doing similar things then try this plan of action.

- Commit yourself to starting the job you are putting off at a definite time. Write this time down.
- If the job or activity is a big one, break it down into smaller jobs which are more manageable. These take less time to complete and seem less daunting.
- Try to get yourself into a rhythm by moving straight from one job to another without giving yourself time to think. By programming yourself almost like a robot to do this, you will achieve far more.
- When you have finished the job, give yourself a small treat. This could be getting a cup of coffee, taking a walk, or having a slice of chocolate cake.

How to motivate yourself

1. Decide a yearly income target for yourself and pin this on the wall directly opposite your desk. Now when you are uncertain about whether to do a job, look at the figure and ask yourself whether doing that job will help you contribute to achieving that figure? Break that income figure down into monthly elements. These may not all be equal amounts if your business is seasonal, or if you intend to allow for summer and Christmas holidays. Try to hit that income figure each month.
2. Put pictures of the things you want up on your wall in front of you and try to get some physical contact with them. Book test drives in cars, test lessons in planes, pick up holiday brochures, try out a new computer.
3. Through your networking, you will have come across others who are starting up in business; so why not agree with them to be 'competitors'; it doesn't matter whether they are in the same business or not. Try to work harder than them and beat the targets you set yourself by more than they beat theirs. You can come to whatever agreement suits the pair of you.

4. Your brain is a powerful tool which is yours to program and enlist help from. It especially likes to think in pictures and you can use this to picture your future success. This is known as 'visualisation'. Begin seeing what you want out of your business (a fast car, good house, holidays abroad, whatever) and do this several times a day for five to ten minutes. Make the pictures as real as you can. After four to five weeks you will find that visualisation gets easier to do. In effect you are programming your subconscious for success. You can adopt this visualisation technique for other elements of your business life, such as seeing yourself make successful sales calls or having an effective meeting where you negotiate what you want.

Overcoming problems working from home

As you've already read, setting up in business at home has many advantages for the young entrepreneur but it also has its downside too. These difficulties have to be overcome if you are to be successful.

The traditional office offers many opportunities to meet people, but if you work from home you will eventually come across the twin problems of loneliness and isolation, which are particularly severe for younger people who are often more sociable than older people. What can you do about this feeling of isolation?

●   Build into your day time to meet people, perhaps by taking a walk to the shops. If you can't do this every day then do it at least twice a week. Don't feel guilty about this. You aren't playing truant but keeping yourself sane and more productive. But make sure you stay 'honest'; set a time when you will be back in the office and at work.

●   If it doesn't disturb your concentration, listen to the radio as you work. Remember to turn it off to take or make telephone calls.

●   Regularly get together with other people who work on their own. You will be creating your own mutual support group; you may even be able to pool resources with other business people so that you can go after bigger contracts.

Managing family and friends

Your family can be very supportive when you set up in business, but when you work from home they can also be particularly disruptive and a major problem. When you work from home, you will come across problems that don't exist at the traditional workplace.

For a start, your family may not like you working from home because it breaks the rhythm and pattern of daily life they have become used to; they just don't like having someone 'under their feet'; and because you run a business from home they think you are just playing at work.

They may also try to take advantage of you by saying such things as 'if you're at home all day, can you do this?' or 'this will only take a minute to do'. Remarks like this show that your family hasn't come to terms with what you are doing.

Preferably, before you even begin working from home, you should firmly establish with the family what you expect of them and they of you. Bringing difficulties out into the open at this early stage will save a lot of aggravation later. Have a family conference and discuss matters. You should have these conferences regularly so that everyone can air their views on how well things are, or aren't, working.

During these conferences, try to create a set of 'ground rules' about what everyone can and cannot do when you start working from home. These rules might include what your office hours are going to be, when your office will be off-limits to younger brothers or sisters perhaps; who can answer the phone during your office hours and what is to be said; and how loud the television is to be during the day.

If there is a clash of interests be prepared to do trade-offs. For example, don't try to stop everyone else from using the phone during the day, but ask them to limit their calls to just ten minutes, rather than talking on and on during your office hours, or offer to have another line put in.

Make your family feel more involved with your work; bounce ideas off them or ask them for their opinions. The more involved they feel, generally the more co-operation you'll get from your family.

Friends and neighbours, as well as family, can also cause problems, just popping by 'because I knew you'd be in', and then want you to make coffee for them, go shopping or nip out to the pub. So you must learn how to say 'no' to them. If you don't, each of these interruptions will cost you money. So when they drop by, explain to them why you can't be disturbed right now and persuade them to phone you in future to find out when you'll be free; then they'll be saved the problem of coming round and finding that you're unavailable.

Plan of action

1. Start acquiring the habit of planning your day, whether it is a work day or a leisure day. The more you do this, the easier it will become.

2. Identify ways in which you waste time regularly. Don't assume that the way you waste time now will be the same ways that you waste time in a month or six months, so keep a check.

3. Identify other entrepreneurs, particularly if you work from home, and arrange to meet with them regularly, to talk over your business problems and to share your experiences.

4. Constantly look for new ways to motivate yourself; use pictures and images of things that you want or want to do.

5. Take every opportunity that you can to make decisions. The more practice you have in this difficult area, the better and faster you will become, resulting in your decision-making becoming easier and more effective.

6. Develop the habit of making sure your desk is clear at the end of every day, not by sweeping everything into the drawers, but by making sure that all the work you intended to do has been done.

9

Taking on Staff

Well, you've set up your business and things seem to be going well. Cash is flowing in, and you're beginning to feel that you could do with a bit of help and you think about employing someone. How do you go about doing that without a great deal of effort and rigmarole?

There are four main reasons why you might want to do this:

- to do work that you don't like doing;
- to do work that you can't do;
- to take over some of the work that you are doing; or
- to free some of your time so you can do higher paid work.

In reality it will probably be for a mixture of these reasons. However, whatever the reason, it is important that right from the start you know what it is that you want your employees to do. If you don't have a pretty clear idea then you'll end up wasting their time and your money, paying them to stand around doing nothing. The following points will help you to decide this.

1. The first thing therefore is to identify the jobs that need to be done. These could range from clerical work to actually making something, doing sales work or driving a van. When you have done that, you will need to work out how long it will take to do each one of these jobs, and how frequently the job has to be done. This will give you a good idea of how much time you will need your employee to work. If it's not going to be a full day or a full week, you may be better off employing someone part-time.

Alternatively, you can ask them to do two different types of job.

2. Now you must work on the practicalities of employing someone. For instance, where will they work? What equipment and materials will they need to do the job? What exactly will be the hours that you need them for? Do they need to be at the office before you or after you?

3. If you work from home, what arrangements are you going to make concerning access? Will you give them a key? If so, after how long? Where will they be allowed to go in the house and what will you allow them to do? Will you want them to work while you are not there? What arrangements are they going to make for lunch?

4. Finally, you will need to decide what their legal status is going to be. Will they be your employees, in which case you will be responsible for their tax and national insurance payments, or will you expect them to work on a freelance or casual basis when they will be responsible for their own tax arrangements?

How to find staff

Having decided what you will want your staff to do, you now have to go out and find them. There are a number of ways of doing this, some perhaps more obvious than others. Initially, why not check close to home for potential employees? Do you have a parent, relative, boyfriend or girlfriend, wife or husband, partner or friend who may be able to take on the job? Better the devil you know, as they say.

If they can't be persuaded to help, do they have any friends who might be able to? Looking close to home is not a waste of time at this stage because you are not only looking for someone who can do the work, but if you are working from home, someone whom you can trust. And being a bit devious, in all honesty it is better to have someone with whom you can take a few liberties at first by asking them to work a few more hours without pay, take on an extra job or two, or even not pay them for a week if things get tight. Your immediate circle might be willing to be temporarily 'abused' in this way when a stranger would not.

If you draw a blank here, contact the local Job Centre and the Careers Service if you want young employees. But do specify as carefully as you can the type of person you want. If you don't you are likely to end up with a succession of totally unsuitable applicants.

Advertising in the local newspaper or putting a card in a shop window if you are only looking for quite low quality staff, can both be cost-effective ways of finding staff.

Whenever you take on strangers, always ask for references and take them up. If people are desperate for a job, they will lie and you don't want to be left in the lurch, or worse still ripped off, and certainly not at this early and crucial stage of your business career.

How to cut your staff costs

The easiest way to do this is to keep them to a minimum right from the start, employing only people when you need them and not paying above the odds for over-qualified staff, unless you know that the job you are asking them to do will soon require their additional skills and experience.

One way of doing this is to pay no salary to a sales person but to make the post commission-only, where the person's income is linked to their success at doing the job.

Alternatively, if you can find someone with the right personality and mix of skills, you might like to work with them on an individual project on a profit basis rather than paying a salary. You will simply split the profits coming from the job. You will of course have to give away more of your potential income to the other person to compensate them for the risk they are taking (the chance that there might not be any profit) and having to wait to be paid (it may be several months before any profits are forthcoming).

How to interview

You'll probably need to interview staff or at least speak to them over the phone before taking them on, but this shouldn't worry you. If you want, think of an interview as a 'getting to know you chat' which makes this sound less formal and more relaxed, which it should be if you want to get a true picture of the interviewee. As a basis use the following plan of action for interviewing.

1. Arrange a time that is convenient for you and at a place you think does the best sales job for you and your company. You could even arrange to meet at a hotel or a pub if you felt that the atmosphere or the environment was more appropriate than your office or home.

2. Expect the interviewee to arrive a little before time. If they don't, mark them down. If they can't turn up on time for a job interview that they supposedly want, they either aren't really interested or are just bad timekeepers. However, if there is a legitimate excuse or reason, do listen to it. Being late could be a one-off thing you should be prepared to forget, if in other respects the interviewee is well suited to the job.

3. Try to get a gut reaction and feeling for them as soon as they arrive. Do they come across as being enthusiastic, friendly and approachable (this is important for sales and reception duties); or are they precise and neat (which is good for administration and accounts)? Do you actually like them?

4. Sit them down and offer them coffee or tea and then spend some time chatting. After five minutes or so, start asking them questions (which you should have written down earlier), about themselves and their experience. You may already know quite a lot about them if they have sent you an application or their curriculum vitae (CV). In particular, ask questions that are relevant to what the person will have to do in their job, such as their experience, skills and how they might handle a certain situation. Don't ask trick questions or try to catch people out.

5. If part of the job will be doing something practical, such as typing, ask the person to take a short test; if you are

going to do this, in all fairness you should tell them that you will expect this when arranging the interview. As they do the test, don't stand over them. Leave them to their own devices and come back in 15 minutes or so. If they haven't been able to do the job (perhaps they don't have the skill and lied to you) don't belittle them, but just say 'that's fine'. The test should be near the end of the interview so at this point you can either continue, if it's worth it, or say goodbye.

6. At the end of your interview day, make a decision about who you will give the job to, or who to call back for further interviews. Don't expect to find the perfect applicant, because you won't; be flexible when choosing. But don't take on just anyone.

Dealing with your staff

When you have taken someone else on board, it is vital that you let them get on with their job. Obviously you will have to spend some time with them at the beginning teaching them the ropes and supervising, but then they must be left to get on with it; otherwise why have them? Of course, if you have chosen your staff wisely, you should seek to delegate as much of your work to them as you can. This will leave you free to do more important things.

How to delegate

There is no point employing staff if you are not going to trust them to do the job, and instead keep on doing it yourself. You therefore need to delegate or pass the work on to your employees by telling your staff clearly and carefully what you want them to do and get their agreement that this is fair and reasonable. Then set a deadline date and time by which the work will be finished.

You should do all of this as early as possible, rather than leaving things right to the last moment because you thought you might be able to do the job and then find you can't. This also helps if any problems arise with a new employee doing the job.

However, if you're not sure they can do the job, either don't give it to them in the first place or do a few early progress checks, which become increasingly further apart, and leave them to it. Once you have delegated the job, let people get on with it. Don't hang around watching them. Trust them and they will do a better job. When the job is over, go through it with them. Talk about what they have done well and what not so well, and why that was.

How to deal with an older employee

If you want experienced staff to do particular jobs, you will probably have to turn to the older employee which can result in a clash for a number of reasons.

An older employee will tend to think that they know better than you, because you are 'green' and 'wet behind the ears'. Of course, there may be some truth in that. There is no point in employing someone for their experience and then not using it; so think carefully about going against their advice. At least listen to it carefully.

However, if you have your own definite ideas about how a job should be done differently, you may find that the older employee thinks they can 'get away with it' and do the job in the way that *they* want to. An explanation of why you are doing the job in that way may sort the problem, backed up by a bit of 'I'm the boss around here' talk, will probably sort the problem out.

If it doesn't, and the situation arises again, then this is one working relationship that probably isn't going to work and it's best if that employee goes. For the same reason, if older employees can't come to terms with any resentment about you having your own business at such a young age, then they too will have to go.

Dealing with young employees

Just as older employees can cause you problems, so can young ones. The problem is here not so much one of 'I know better than you', but is more likely to be a lack of respect for your authority. Again, if you can't win their respect they will have to go. An explanation that this is the case will often sort the issue out.

Your legal obligations

Whenever you employ staff, even those on a casual basis, you are entering into a potential legal minefield which cannot possibly be covered in the space available in this book. So before embarking on your quest for staff, talk to your solicitor about the possible implications for you and read up on the subject of employment law.

Plan of action

1. When you have determined what you want staff to do, write out a short description of the person you want to take the job. This should include the main activities you want them to do and the skills they will need to do this.

2. Now make a second list of all the other skills that it would be very useful for them to have but which are not essential. This will not only help you to decide between two closely matched candidates, but it will also provide you with some flexibility if you decide to take your business in other directions.

3. Read as much as you can on employment law and requirements.

4. Contact the local Job Centre and find out their procedures for hiring staff through them.

10

Sources of Information

There are many organisations and groups around the country, all designed to help the would-be and new entrepreneur. However, few of them are aimed at the younger business person, though two very important ones are. Both Livewire and the Prince's Youth Business Trust have local and regional offices. They can supply information, advice and in some cases finance. Contact their head offices:

Livewire
Hawthorn House
Forth Banks
Newcastle upon Tyne NE1 3SG
Tel: 0345 573252 (local call rate)

The Prince's Youth Business Trust
5th Floor
5 Cleveland Place
London SW1Y 6JJ
Tel: 0171 321 6500

Training and Enterprise Councils (TECs) in England and Wales and **Local Enterprise Companies** (LECs) in Scotland offer free advisory and counselling services, as well as running business training courses.

You can obtain the name and address of your nearest one from the local Jobcentre.

Organisations useful to the new business

Association of British Insurers (ABI), 51 Gresham Street, London EC2V 7HQ; Tel: 0171 600 3333

British Insurance and Investment Brokers Association, BIIBA House, 14 Bevis Marks, London EC3A 7NT; Tel: 0171 623 9043

British Venture Capital Association, 3 Catherine Place, London SW1E 6DX; Tel: 0171 233 5212

Business in the Community, 8 Stratton Street, London W1X 5FD; Tel: 0171 629 1600

In Scotland:
Scottish Business in the Community, Romano House, 43 Station Road, Corstorphine, Edinburgh EH12 7AF; Tel: 0131 334 9876

They can supply the address of your local Enterprise Agency: such agencies offer independent business advice and information. They may be able to provide help with training and premises.

Capital Exchange, PO Box 127, Hereford HR4 0YN; Tel: 01432 342484

Credit reference agencies:

Dun and Bradstreet, 4 Bonhill Street, London EC2A 4BU; Tel: 0171 256 8733

Equifax Europe, Spectrum House, 1A North Avenue, Clydebank, Glasgow G81 2DR; Tel: 0141 951 1100

Graydon UK Ltd, Hyde House, Edgware Road, London NW9 6LW; Tel: 0181 975 1050

Ethnic Minority Business Development Unit, Calcutta House, Old Castle Street, London E1 7NT; Tel: 0171 283 1030

Federation of Small Businesses, 32 Orchard Road, Lytham St Annes, Lancashire FY8 1NY; Tel: 01253 720911

Finance and Leasing Association, 18 Upper Grosvenor Street, London W1X 9PB; Tel: 0171 491 2783

The Forum of Private Business, Ruskin Chambers, Drury Lane, Knutsford, Cheshire WA16 6HA; Tel: 01565 634467

Health and Safety Executive, Baynards House, Chepstow Place, London W2 4TF; Tel: 0171 243 6000

Instant Muscle, Springside House, 84 North End Road, London W14 9ES; Tel: 0171 603 2604

Institute of Chartered Accountants in England and Wales, PO Box 433, Chartered Accountants' Hall, Moorgate Place, London EC2P 2BJ; Tel: 0171 920 8682

Institute of Chartered Accountants of Scotland, 27 Queen Street, Edinburgh EH2 1LA; Tel: 0131 225 5673

Institute of Management, Small Firms Information Service, Management House, Cottingham Road, Corby, Northamptonshire NN17 1TT; Tel: 01536 204222

The Law Society, 113 Chancery Lane, London WC2A 1PL; Tel: 0171 242 1222

Local Investment Networking Company (LINC), 4 Snow Hill, London EC1A 2BS; Tel: 0171 236 3000

Registrar of Companies, Companies Registration Office, Crown Way, Cardiff DF4 3UZ; Tel: 01222 388588

Royal British Legion, 48 Pall Mall, London SW1Y 5JY; Tel: 0171 973 0633

Rural Development Commission, 141 Castle Street, Salisbury, Wiltshire SP1 3TP; Tel: 01722 336255

Telecottage Association, Wren Telecottage, Stoneleigh Park, Warwickshire CV8 2RR; Tel: 01203 696986

Publications

Business magazines are available from newsagents or on subscription. The following titles are likely to be of interest to the readers of this book.

Business Age; monthly. On subscription from: VNU Business

Publications, VNU House, 32–34 Broadwick Street, London W1E 6EZ; Tel: 0171 316 9000.

Business Opportunity World; monthly. From newsagents.

Enterprise; monthly. On subscription from: Selous House, 5–12 Mandela Street, London NW1; Tel: 0171 916 1880.

Home Run; ten times a year. On subscription from: 79 Black Lion Lane, London W6 9BG; Tel: 0181 846 9244.

There are innumerable books on starting and running a business; a selection is listed below. Full details of Kogan Page small business publications is available on application to: 120 Pentonville Road, London N1 9JN; Tel: 0171 278 0433; Fax 0171 837 6348.

Starting a business

Be Your Own Boss: The Daily Express Guide, David Mc Mullen. Kogan Page, 1994

How to Set Up and Run Your Own Business: The Daily Telegraph Guide. Kogan Page, annual

Great Ideas for Making Money: The Daily Express Guide, Niki Chesworth. Kogan Page, 1994

The Lloyds Bank Small Business Guide, Sara Williams, Penguin, 9th edition, 1995

Working for Yourself: The Daily Telegraph Guide, Godfrey Golzen. Kogan Page, annual

Getting Started, Robson Rhodes. Kogan Page, 4th edition, 1995

Your image

The Image Factor, Eleri Sampson. Kogan Page, 1994

Your Total Image: How to Communicate Success, Philippa Davies. Piatkus, 1990

Working from home

How to Work from Home, Ian Phillipson. How to Books, 1992

Running a Home-Based Business, Diane M Baker. Kogan Page, 1994

Communication

How to Communicate Effectively, Bert Decker. Kogan Page, 1989
How to Develop a Positive Attitude, Elwood N Chapman. Kogan Page, 1988
Readymade Business Letters that Get Results: The Daily Express Guide, Jim Douglas. 2nd edition, Kogan Page, 1994

Getting things done

Getting Things Done, Roger Black. Michael Joseph, 1987
How to Develop a Positive Attitude, Elwood N Chapman. Kogan Page, 1988
How to Develop Assertiveness, Sam R Lloyd. Kogan Page, 1988
Make Every Minute Count, Marion E Haynes. Kogan Page, 1988
101 Ways to Clean Up Your Act, Dianna Booher. Kogan Page, 1994

Sales and marketing

How to Do Your Own PR, Ian Phillipson. How to Books, 1995
How to Sell More: The Daily Express Guide, Neil Johnson. Kogan Page, 1994
Marketing for the Small Business, Derek Waterworth. Macmillan Educational, 1987
The Secrets of Telephone Selling, Neil Johnson. Kogan Page, 1994
Prospecting for Customers, Robert Vicar. Kogan Page, 1993
Successful Marketing for the Small Business: The Daily Telegraph Guide, Dave Patten. Kogan Page, 3rd edition, 1995

Finance and accounts

How to Prepare a Business Plan, Edward Blackwell. Kogan Page, 2nd edition, 1993
Business Plans, Brian Finch. Kogan Page, 1992
Financial Management for the Small Business, Colin Barrow. Kogan Page, 3rd edition, 1995
Guide to Grants for Business, ed M Martin. Associated Management Services, 1995
Do Your Own Bookkeeping, Max Pullen. Kogan Page, 1988

Index